The Guru Method

Essays

For information contact:

Michael Tan
GSMS Education Pty Ltd
P.O Box 3848
Marsfield NSW
2122
Australia

TABLE OF CONTENTS

INTRODUCTION 4

TOPIC ONE 5

ESSAYS AND ANALYSES FROM TOPIC ONE.............................. 6-22

TOPIC TWO.. 23

ESSAYS AND ANALYSES FROM TOPIC TWO 24-51

TOPIC THREE.. 52

ESSAYS AND ANALYSES FROM TOPIC THREE 53-65

TOPIC FOUR 66

ESSAYS AND ANALYSES FROM TOPIC FOUR 67-73

TOPIC FIVE 74

ESSAYS AND ANALYSES FROM TOPIC FIVE 75-88

TOPIC SIX.. 89

ESSAYS AND ANALYSES FROM TOPIC SIX 90-99

INTRODUCTION

I introduced the Guru Method Essay analysis service in 2008, what I noticed is that most people didn't know where to begin in terms of writing a Section II GAMSAT essay.

What I have compiled here in this book is a selection of actual student essays written by GAMSAT candidates and the accompanying analysis. These essays are NOT "model" essays to copy but are selected to illustrate common mistakes and errors that are made by candidates in their essay writing.

Use the essays and analyses in this book as a tool to reflect on your own essay writing tendencies. The combination of this book and my Essay analysis service will give you the most effective Section II preparation any GAMSAT candidate will have.

Michael Tan

Here follow the 6 topics that candidates were asked to write an essay on.

ESSAY TOPICS: TOPIC ONE

TOPIC ONE

Consider the following comments and develop a piece of writing in response to one or more of them.

Your writing will be judged on the quality of your response to the theme; how well you organise and present your point of view, and how effectively you express yourself.

You will not be judged on the views or attitudes you express.

* * * * * * *

Ability is of little account without opportunity.

Napoleon Bonaparte

The fox has many tricks. The hedgehog has but one. But that is the best of all.

Desiderius Erasmus

As we advance in life we learn the limits of our abilities.

James A. Froude

To know how to hide one's ability is great skill.

Francois de la Rochefoucauld

The winds and waves are always on the side of the ablest navigators.

Edward Gibbon

ESSAYS AND ANALYSES: TOPIC ONE

....

ESSAY ONE

"Ability is of little account without opportunity".

Napoleon Bonaparte

What is an opportunity?

It is no doubt that Napoleon Bonaparte is a great man with great ability. The ability to lead, use of tactic and strategy to win the French Revolution. The ability to change and re-shape French history. As Napoleon once said "As the world perish, I was born", to him that was an opportunity because he born at the right time and place. It often said that war time create hero, and Bonaparte was one of those hero. While it is not a debatable matter that ability is of little account without opportunity, however, the aspect of opportunity is a debatable matter.

Martin Luther King is the first African-American to stand up and voice against the discrimination and racism. The first person to challenge the government, those in authority and those who are racism. The first to ask for equality among all citizen of American. It is no doubt that his great charisma skill and the speech "I have a dream" have moved the heart of millions of American. He took the opportunity to speak for himself and on behalf of millions of African-American, with years of fighting and an endless effort to achieve it.

What if the opportunity does not come? Is it then that their ability is still of little account? I believe that one can still achieve greatness even if they were not given an opportunity. Bill Gates once applied for a job at IBM, but his application was refused. He was not given an opportunity to demonstrate his expert programming skill. What should he do? Should he wait for another opportunity to come by maybe in the next ten years or should he create his own opportunity? Then, he team up with a friend to build the first Microsoft Windows, which has revolutionise computing technology. Yes! Opportunity can be create.

There were also people who with no doubt have great ability, but were not given an opportunity neither were they able to create an opportunity. As in the case of Nelson Mandela, who tried to bring peace, equality and welfare for people of Africa. His voice was suppressed when he was sent to life imprisonment for more than two decades. They have managed to silence his voice, but what he had said and done still live in many people hearts and mind. What he tried to achieve is not for himself but for everyone. His altruistic motives had started the fire, although he could not made any changes due to his imprisonment, but it will be a matter of time before change start to occur and take shape. Although, he was later release and elect as president of South Africa because of many campaign worldwide to ask for his release; an opportunity finally comes. The point is if the person has altruistic motives for his action, reassure that his action is the first step for a thousand miles journey, regardless of whether they fail or succeed in making a change.

In conclusion, ability can be of little account without an opportunity but opportunity does not always mean you have to be there at the right time and place, and its does not have to be given by someone. "When an opportunity come, seize it with all your ability, if it does not come, then try to create your own opportunity".

THOUGHT AND CONTENT

Strengths

Interpreting your chosen quote, and developing your own thought-provoking theory on the basis of that interpretation shows originality.

Areas for Improvement

Your first two paragraphs are extremely weak because they do not serve the purpose of introducing your thesis (the main point of your essay). In fact, instead of enhancing your essay, those two paragraphs detract from it.

It is not until the final sentence of your conclusion that the reader actually knows the point you apparently intended to make, as follows:

"When an opportunity come, seize it with all your ability, if it does not come, then try to create your own opportunity".

Suggestions

(1) Let the reader know the point you want to make early on, preferably in the first paragraph. (See more about this later, under the "Organisation and Expression" portion of this analysis, below.)

(2) Avoid exaggerated, dramatic claims that are totally inaccurate and as a result make your work look like something a middle school child would write, such as this sentence from your second paragraph:

Martin Luther King is the first African-American to stand up and voice against the discrimination and racism. The first person to challenge the government, those in authority and those who are racism. The first to ask for equality among all citizen of American.

The Rev. King was actively speaking out in the 1960's, one hundred years after the slaves were freed by the Emancipation Proclamation. Your claim seems to say that you think no one ever spoke out against the continuing racism in the United States during that entire period of 100 years! If you do not know the history of an issue, it is better not to provide historical examples at all.

ORGANISATION AND EXPRESSION

Strengths

Your writing conveys the strength of your own convictions.

Areas for Improvement

(1) Statement of thesis: Although you finally got around to letting the reader know what you wanted to write about, waiting until the end was a big flaw. Your position should be stated clearly at the outset, to orient the reader, as well as let readers know why they should be interested in reading further....

(2) The lack of proper organisation of this essay is evidence of lack of planning. Instead of a clear thesis right at the outset, followed by a well-reasoned line of thought developed from the basic premise, you have written something that looks like a letter you might write to a friend. In a communication like that, we write down whatever comes into our head, without worrying about planning how to build a case.

Suggestions

(1) Remember, when you are writing an argumentative essay, you are building a case, which you are going to use to convince your reader, just as an attorney does in a courtroom in order to convince the judge and/or jury. As you can see, the suggestion here is that you examine every idea and every sentence that you think of during the planning stage, making sure each and every one you include contributes to your argument.

(2) For your next argumentative essay: First things first. Try to master the standard, basic 5-paragraph structure of an argumentative essay: The first paragraph introduces the thesis and makes brief mention of two or three supporting examples. Then, in the following 2 or 3 paragraphs, each of those supporting examples just mentioned is fleshed out, with specific explanation of how each example supports the main thesis. Finally, the concluding paragraph wraps up the essay, and possibly includes speculation of what the future might hold with regard to the subject of the essay.

(3) This is a minor point, but nevertheless something you should pay attention to: Your

concerning sentence, which — as was mentioned earlier — seems to serve as the only real formulation of your thesis, has quotation marks around it. Whose words are those? Are they yours? If so, you should not have enclosed them in quotation marks. What it means, when quotation marks are used to enclose a remark that a person has made, is that you are quoting the exact words of <u>someone else.</u> This is very important in academic sorts of writing, because it is not proper to use someone else's words without mentioning who wrote them. On the other hand, if that sentence is yours, and you want it to stand out, you can use underlining, or italics, but never quotation marks.

The one single promising way to improve your next essay:

Study the two essay formats (argumentative and reflective) as outlined in your study guide, "The Guru Method," especially pages 6-23.

ESSAY TWO

Ability is of little account without opportunity. This quote by Napoleon Bonaparte is a valid observation in today's society. With exposure and resources, those that are able to develop some skill are facilitated to succeed. Socioeconomically disadvantaged people may have some skill or talent in a field, but be unable to use it in a useful way due to lack of opportunity. If one is truly talented at something however, they can find a way to become exposed even when obstacles present.

Opportunity allows people to become able at various activities. Money, time, exposure and effort allow people to become skilled at things even if no natural talent previously existed. A private school education for example, exposes children to activities such as rowing, music and performing arts. This allows these children to try things they would not normally try and become skilled at the ones they choose to. With minimal opportunity, exposure to various activities is reduced thus decreasing the chance of discovery of ability.

There is no point in being good at something when there is no opportunity to use it in some way that is useful. One could be the most talented writer in the world, but if no one ever gets to read this writing, what is the point? Many people of a disadvantaged background may have special skills in activities that are performed in daily life. These may include basketball, football, singing, writing or running, because these can be performed without having resources like money, sports grounds, or musical instruments. This potential talent goes to waste in a society that often does not give opportunity for this minority.

An optimistic person may believe that true talent overcomes all barriers. If someone has particular skill or natural ability at something, maybe destiny intervenes such that they find success. Reality television shows that showcase singing often demonstrate the ability of people that have never had the opportunity to perform, and this can result in successful careers. The odds of this happening however are low, and there is no substitute for resources, exposure and effort in developing a skill and becoming successful.

Opportunity allows ability to be developed and to shine. With opportunity, people are facilitated to become successful. Intuition and natural talent are often left unseen and thus those without opportunity are not allowed to succeed the way others are. Sometimes one that is truly talented can find a way to become exposed even when obstacles present. However, our society favours those with opportunity causing these people to succeed with their abilities with more ease than the disadvantaged

THOUGHT AND CONTENT

Strengths

Your line of thought shows promise: your earnest attempt to formulate a creative, original response to the relatively commonplace wisdom of the quote you chose is evident.

Areas for Improvement

This essay leaves the reader wondering, "And your point is…..?" Your introductory paragraph, which should introduce the main theme you want to get across, provides a statement that seems to do just that:

If one is truly talented at something however, they can find a way to become exposed even when obstacles present.

OK, that's a statement of strong belief in the ability of truly talented individuals to overcome the obstacles, and does stimulate the reader to want to know more….

However, by the penultimate paragraph, the reader, whose disappointment has already been growing, sees this discouraging remark:

.,,,, The odds of this happening however are low,…

and the final blow comes in the concluding paragraph:

Sometimes one that is truly talented can find a way to become exposed even when obstacles present. However,…….

At this point, instead of having convinced the reader of the validity of your inspiring message that the truly talented will find a way (and, it seems to suggest, always will), you've demolished your own premise by arriving at the much more moderate (and probably more valid) conclusion that this only happens *sometimes*.

Suggestions

Remember that in an argumentative essay, the argument (or "thesis") takes center stage. Once you've decided on it and then carefully worded it in your thesis statement at the outset, it is important to remain focused on it throughout the essay.

Remember the elements necessary for writing an argumentative essay, as succinctly outlined in "The Guru Method:" "An argumentative essay requires you to evaluate the validity of the quotation, take a position, explain it and use reasons to consolidate it."

Note that this is very different from writing in a journalistic or reporting style, which you seem to have attempted in this piece; that style encourages the writer to be as objective as possible by exploring both sides of an issue as fairly as possible.

ORGANISATION AND EXPRESSION

Strengths

The structural framework, in terms of the order in which you present your material, is basically sound.

Areas for Improvement

In general, the essay is quite repetitive, due to the repeated use of the same words over and over in each paragraph.

The fact is that you make all your important points in the form of generalities about human behavior throughout, and therefore, to put it brutally but honestly, your essay reads like a dull textbook.

Suggestions

Enhance your discussion by putting some real people into the picture. Whenever you come across a piece of writing that has as its central theme some aspect of human behavior, but only speaks about it in generalities, such as "people tend to do this or that," and never refers to any specific people as examples to make its point — you are looking at a piece of writing that's guaranteed to bore you

The one single promising way to improve your next essay:

Keep your target audience in mind: Whenever you write anything in your lifetime (except for personal journals you don't intend to show anyone, ever), you should keep in mind the nature and values of the reader you intend to reach. In the case of these essays, you are aiming at the person who will evaluate your work and give you a mark for it.

That person is likely to be an academic with relatively broad knowledge in a number of fields, perhaps a bit skeptical. Although you do need to keep in mind that this person will be looking for quality of thought (otherwise known as "depth of thought"), it is certainly true as well that he/she is human. That means he/she will be looking for something just plain interesting and credible -- possibly also refreshing, something that makes him/her go on thinking over what you've said for some time after reading it. Or perhaps, after reading it, saying simply, "I never thought of it that way,"

ESSAY THREE

"Ability is of little account without opportunity"

Napoleon Bonaparte.

"Time and tide waits for no man". In simple terms, 'Ability' is the innate quality of a human being to complete the task with great efficiency. Opportunity is that once chance which can take this ability to a whole new level. Human beings function at different levels of efficiency and given the chance to function at this higher level opens them up to a whole new world of possibilities. Once they are at this level, possibilities are endless. They can use this opportunity to attain their main goals in life, whether it is to benefit themselves, their family or to benefit the community. As a matter of fact, it is proven that <u>ability is of little account without an opportunity</u>.

Take the life of the Oscar winning actor, Angelina Jolie. I believe it is one of the best examples we can relate to in this discussion. She is a very able actor and a social worker. She had the innate artistic ability and she was given the opportunity to present it with the break she got into the movies due to the influence of her Oscar winning actor-father. She gave every opportunity that came knocking by her door, the best shot. She never missed an opportunity to excel. She used her money to benefit herself, her family and the wider community. She is actively involved in humanitarian acts in the third world countries, being the United Nations' Goodwill Ambassador. It is not often that such life-changing opportunities come knocking by. There were other actors as well who had similar opportunities in life but never utilised it for the good of others or even did justice to their ability. People like her used this opportunity to fight against the plague of poverty and its consequences like poor health and hygiene in developing nations, and to emphasise the importance of education for the upcoming generation.

At the same time, we have aspiring artists of similar ability, waiting for the one opportunity. They wake up every day hoping for that one chance to make a difference. They are all waiting for that one opportunity to showcase their talents but they end up not getting that one break which people like Jolie got in their lives. This could be because of their low socio-economic background and their upbringing.

On the other hand, some people create opportunities by tirelessly exploring the different possibilities to succeed or achieve their goals in life. Sometimes, we need to create the opportunity by our dogged hardwork and iron will. They wait for that one break, the opportunity, like a predator waiting for its prey to err. "Hard work beats talent when Talent doesn't work hard". These people view every day as an opportunity. We had a couple of young art students visiting us with a big set of amazing oil paintings. They were promoting their art, raising money for art students like them and for charity, but at the same time trying to find that passionate art lover in one of their hosts to give them a life changing opportunity. Such opportunity is hard to come by; so their ability is not known to the broader community.

Think of man's first step on Moon in July 1969. Neil Armstrong had the ability but had Neil Armstrong not seized that opportunity, what would have been the case? That would have been a lost opportunity and a valid reason to regret for the rest of his life. It all comes to these famous words by Neil Armstrong after he set foot on Moon.

"One small step for a man, a giant leap for mankind".

THOUGHT AND CONTENT

Strengths

With regard to the line of thought you were attempting to convey, you clearly had some good points that were well thought out. This indicates that if you take to heart the suggestions for improvement that follow in this analysis, with special attention to planning your thought line carefully and organising your presentation in a cohesive manner, you may very well have a bright future in essay writing

Areas for Improvement

In planning an argumentative essay, your aim should be first, to decide what your position (your "argument") is going to be, and then to make a clear thesis statement as early as possible, followed by examples and evidence to support your position—in other words, you should then lay out reasons why you've made that thesis statement.

Your thesis statement for this essay appears to be: *As a matter of fact, it is proven that ability is of little account without an opportunity.* That is a very emphatic statement, using strong terms such as "fact" and "proven," and you provide, as evidence to support your argument, a total of one example of a real person, Ms. Jolie. That's OK, so far, so good, she's indeed an example of a talented person seizing opportunity.

However, in the absence of a definition of the antiquated phrase "of little account," the reader is left wondering about all those nameless others, including those art students you mention. Presumably, since they are still waiting for "that one opportunity," then they must be *of little account.* But what does that mean? If we compare them to Ms. Jolie, who has a successful career and is an active humanitarian, are we to understand that those poor souls who are still waiting for opportunity are essentially failures? Are they of little account because they are not monetarily successful. Or, although they are good at what they do but are failures because *their ability is not known to the broader community,* does that mean they are not contributing to society in any way?

What about people who have ability but aren't looking for opportunity – and even turn down opportunity when it pops up — because they want to be able enjoy their ability and the value it brings them —in privacy. How about a musician who was a prodigy as a child, but at the age of 10 decided he hated all the pressure of concerts, etc., and is now 35, practices his music privately, still enjoys his ability for its own sake immensely, etc....is his ability of little account, whatever that means?

Suggestions

Learn the two types of essay formats that have been suggested for this course. Follow the guidelines for writing an argumentative essay or a reflective essay, as provided in the study guide, "The Guru Method." These guidelines have been worked out specifically to aid you in those difficult moments when you are facing an exam and have a very short time to write a convincing piece of writing. The idea behind sticking to one of those 2 formats is so that you can avoid panic when you are sitting for the exam, and instead can feel confident because you have practiced writing both these types.

ORGANISATION AND EXPRESSION

Strengths

Your mastery of English, in terms of your writing skills such as sentence structure and vocabulary, is at quite an advanced level, and therefore your writing conveys the strength of your own convictions.

Areas for Improvement

Defining terms is always helpful in any essay, but essential when the terms are archaic or in a foreign language. In this essay, definitions were provided for *ability* and for *opportunity*. All well and good; *ability* and *opportunity* are words that are in our present-day vocabulary, but nevertheless, providing your own definition is helpful, as it helps your reader understand your interpretation of the quote you chose.

Unfortunately, however, you failed to define the most important item of all,

which is the phrase "of little account." Napoleon probably made his remark in French some 200 years ago, and it seems obvious that the translation of it in the quote supplied for this practice essay dates from that period. That is, the English is 200 years old. The words "ability" and "opportunity" that you did define are still in use, but the phrase "of little account" is not. And yet you chose to highlight that phrase by using it in your thesis statement. That is why the criticism is made, above, in such detail, about your failure to define that phrase. Instead of letting the reader know what your interpretation of that archaic phrase is –which would help very much—you leave the reader to feeling in a muddle.

Also, the essay wanders. For example, the entire section about people creating opportunities seems to contradict your earlier notions. Indeed, the section begins with the phrase *On the other hand*, which confuses because it detracts from your argument. Remember, in an argumentative essay you are not trying to examine an issue from all sides; if that were the case, then it would be fine to launch into an "on the other hand" discussion. But you're writing an essay, not a report.

Suggestions

Try to curb your tendency to exaggerate. Here are two examples of exaggeration: one is your use of the phrase *it is proven*." What proof are you referring to? The other instance is found in the paragraph on Ms. Jolie: *She gave every opportunity that came knocking by her door, the best shot. She never missed an opportunity to excel.* Your reader must assume you do not know Ms. Jolie personally, and that therefore you have no way of knowing whether these statements are true, or perhaps the opposite is true: maybe her mailbox and voicemail have always been flooded with tons of opportunities, and she turned down all of them except the one that would make her the most money or bring her into the brightest spotlight.

You are writing an argumentative essay for a serious-minded audience of academics — or, more specifically, one academic: the person who will mark your essay. That person is looking for a thoughtful attempt to convince him or her of your point, not a sales pitch. So, claims that sound like wild exaggeration have a detrimental effect.

The one single promising way to improve your next essay:

PLAN, PLAN, PLAN Take at least 5 minutes to plan before you start the actual writing.

For an argumentative essay, spend the time to formulate a thesis statement and then stick to it like glue. This is how planning works: Step 1: What is my position, my claim? OK, I've got that -- now put it into a thesis statement. 2. OK, now I've got a sentence saying what i think. 3. Why do I think that? What is my supporting evidence?

Reason 1. Reason 2. (Maybe even Reason 3). Each one of those reasons gets a separate paragraph stating the reason, and then examples of the reason. After that, the conclusion is easy.

ESSAY FOUR

As we advance in life we learn the limits of our abilities.   (James A. Froude)

There are some truths in the quote above by James A. Froude that 'as we advance in life, we learn the limits of our abilities'. However, this does not mean that once we had learnt about our limitations, we cannot progress to the next level with our abilities.

As we grow, in addition to discovering our natural talents, we do take up learned abilities along the way through the influence of people that we encounter, the circumstances that unfold in our lives and also the education systems that most civilised societies provide. Some may take longer to harness their abilities to a competent level, while some may become experts in a short period of time due to their natural aptitude and their innate talents. Thus, every person progresses differently in their abilities depending on each individual's aptitude level and the only way for a person to know how one is faring is by comparing one's ability with either another's similar ability or comparing with the benchmarks set by specific groups or institutions.

That being said, opportunity does play a major role in allowing one's ability to be discovered, grow and flourish. Without it, any ability (whether known or unknown) that one has, one may never know the full potential of one's ability in his or her whole lifetime. However, a person's circumstance may limit the accessibility of opportunities. Take for instance, if two youths are musically gifted, the one who comes from an influential and wealthy background will have more and easily available opportunities in pursuing his or her musical talent like able to purchase the required instrument to practise on, able to apply to attend any prestigious music schools or institutions with ease, as compared to the other youth who comes from a not so-well –to-do background.

Nevertheless, regardless of one's financial background, any person without a supportive environment to grow up in would end up with a diminished sense of ability. Hence, a positive mindset and a determined attitude developed generally from a supportive upbringing would bring out the best in people to reach and aim high and these individuals will seek or/and create their opportunities to accomplish their goals. A very good and inspiring example would be James R. Doty M.D (Professor of Neurosurgery, Stanford University School of Medicine) who was interviewed by Steve Cannane on 'The Drum' TV show (aired on 1 November 2012 on ABC News), defied the norm where he as a youth coming from a dysfunctional family, who had not the means or any idea of even ever thinking of getting into college and being someone, was able to become a neurosurgeon. His secret to success was due to the teachings regarding meditation of the mind and the power of positive thinking, from a very kind elderly woman who he was fortunate to meet in a magic shop at the age of 13. That single meeting had a profound effect that changed his perspective and transformed his outlook from limited possibilities to unlimited possibilities. Hence, by age 19, even though his grades were well below the average acceptance level for medical colleges, he was brave enough to demand a meeting with the heads of that college and argued his way in, where finally the pre-medical committee wrote a very good recommendation letter for him to be accepted into that medical school. Thus, he created his own opportunity and the rest was history.

In conclusion, with a continues positive mindset, passion, perseverance, creativity and with some imagination, I believe that there will be no limit in one's ability as he or she is dedicated in learning and striving to be above any standards to achieve the extraordinary and the impossible for the rest of his or her life.

THOUGHT AND CONTENT

Strengths

The line of thought you built on the basis of your interpretation of the Froude quote came through to the reader clearly by the end of the essay.

Areas for Improvement

The essay is seriously flawed by the fact that, although you did indeed present your view, the reader only discerns it at the end of the essay, in the concluding paragraph. Up to that point, what you wrote was a wandering discussion, not an essay. From the beginning of the piece, you appeared to be attempting to examine, from all sides, the notion expressed by the author of the quote.

In order to understand this critique, it's vital that you understand the purpose of any essay. When you write in this format, your job is not to discuss, nor to examine, nor to be fair and objective. The word "essay" is derived from ancient French; it meant "to try." The purpose of an essay is to try to convince the reader that your point of view on a particular topic is valid.

The most effective way to do this is to state your point of view (your thesis) at the outset of the essay, and then proceed to set forth reasons (usually in the form of examples) to support your thesis. In your piece, you never got around to your thesis until the 4th paragraph, with the sentence that begins *Hence, a positive mindset and a determined attitude*— and then you used the rest of that overlong paragraph giving only one, quite overlong supporting example.

After that one example of a person succeeding against mighty odds, you followed up with the aforementioned thesis statement (which you only provided in the conclusion, whereas it should have been in the introductory paragraph). This is why the essay is unconvincing — one example of a highly motivated person (who was unusual in so many ways) succeeding is simply not enough.

Suggestions

Now that you know the importance of establishing a thesis, make sure that before you start to write anything, you do two things: work out the thesis in a sentence or two in your mind, and then work out a complete plan for the essay. See more about this under the heading "Organisation and Expression," below.

ORGANISATION AND EXPRESSION

Strengths

Your greatest strength in the "Expression" category is the story about the neurosurgeon. Although it was criticized above as being too long, that does not negate the fact that it was essentially an engaging story that not only made for easy reading, but also served as evidence for your thesis.

Areas for Improvement

Whenever you come across a piece of writing that has as its central theme some aspect of human behaviour, but only speaks about it in generalities, such as "people tend to do this or that," and never refers to any specific people as examples to make its point -- you are looking at a piece of writing that's guaranteed to bore you. Your essay was a striking example of this, and here is the proof: an actual word count shows that you wrote exactly 100 more words about people in the abstract than about real persons (362 words from the first word of the essay to the word *Hence,* and only 262 words from that point to the end).

Suggestions

Consider the elements necessary for writing an argumentative essay, as succinctly outlined in "The Guru Method:" "An argumentative essay requires you to evaluate the validity of the quotation, take a position, explain it and use reasons to consolidate it." Focus on pages 6-23 of "the Guru Method."

Familiarize yourself with the two types of essay format outlined in "The Guru Method," especially pages 6-23. While the Gamsat does not require any particular format be used, the idea behind learning these two is that when you are under the limited time pressure of the actual test, you will be able to rely on a proven format that you have practiced and perfected.

The one single promising way to improve your next essay:

Plan, plan, plan. For an argumentative essay, spend the time to plan, plan, plan -- formulate a thesis statement and then stick to it like glue. This is how planning works: Step 1: What is my position, my claim? OK, I've got that -- now put it into a thesis statement. 2. OK, now I've got a sentence saying what i think. Why do I think that? Reason 1. Reason 2. (Maybe even Reason 3). Each one of those reasons gets a separate paragraph stating the reason, and then providing examples of the reason. After that, the conclusion is easy; it's a wrap-up, and may include hope for the future.

ESSAY FIVE

Ability is of little account without opportunity – Napoleon Bonaparte

One should be provided with ample opportunities in life to show off their ability or skill-set. These opportunities can be in times of social gatherings, in times of need or for the general success of one's ambitions and goals.

I can relate to the time I tried getting into the Indian Institute of Technology, which is generally considered the best place to study Chemical Engineering. As a young aspirant, I had to write plenty of entrance examinations to simply prove that I would be a great candidate. This seemed unfair, as I had to do a series of tests that had nothing to do with the actual program, and I was not being given an opportunity to prove my intelligence in the university degree.

Conversely, my brother had an experience that changed his perception of opportunity. He had the perfect opportunity to display his ability, for a good cause too. As an avid player of Flight Simulator X on his computer, he had a basic understanding of flight controls and communication protocol over radio. Once when we were on a domestic flight while holidaying in Nepal, the co-pilot had a stroke and was unable to continue duty. The pilot had to steer his fifty-odd passengers alone to safety, if not for my brother, Alex. This warranted a search by the cabin crew for someone on the plane who had an understanding of flight controls. This was needed to assist the captain in communicating and entering flight parameters while the captain through to the nearest airport amidst the Himalayas successfully. This landed him with recognition from the aviation boards of Nepal and the United States for his valuable assistance; leading him to his dream job of becoming a commercial pilot.

This shows how without an opportunity, it may not be possible to show your skills to the world. Your ability is what counts at the end of the day, provided you have the one opportunity to capitalise on.

THOUGHT AND CONTENT

Strengths

Your line of thought shows promise: your attempt to formulate a creative, relevant response to the quote you chose is evident.

Areas for Improvement

The true "area for improvement" is actually no just one area, but rather the entire piece of writing. This is because this attempt at a reflective essay is not thought-provoking. It simply tells a story, except for the last three lines of the very last paragraph of the essay. In those lines, you're finally, going in the right direction, but it's just not enough. The essay is out of balance – you've told a story in great detail and ended up with a very, very brief – too brief -- summary of your reflections of an experience — an experience that was not even your own. The essay should have been the other way around, with a very brief description of the event, and a much longer section where you should have expanded on how the experience — preferably an experience of your own – and why you feel it is important, how it might have changed you.

The absence of "quality of thought" of the entire essay is the underlying weakness of this piece of writing. The basic concepts of the essay are clear and easily understood; while this is always desirable in an essay, it alone is not enough to make an essay rise above average. There is no real depth of thought.

What you have done is truly ironic. While you claim that: *I was not being given an opportunity to prove my intelligence in the university degree* —in this very same piece of writing in which you bemoan the absence of opportunity in the past, you have actually passed up an opportunity to show your intellectual ability in the present! That is what both the practice essays and the Gamsat itself offer you: the opportunity to showcase that ability -- a quality which is weighted very heavily in the marking of the Gamsat (about 75%).

Suggestions

You are advised to consult the study guide, "The Guru Method," especially pages 6-23." It may be that if you did read the portion about reflective essays, you only skimmed it, and missed the point. Perhaps you picked up on the idea that you can write about a personal experience, and you may have liked that idea so well that you ignored the sentence that explains the difference between an argumentative essay and a reflective one. It's worth quoting the main point here: "A reflective essay is still an argument...."Understand that some attention to specific details is crucial. However, DO NOT tell stories – they should only serve as take-off points for reflecting on the experience...

How did these experiences create meaning for you? What reasons had led you to your experience or your behaviour? What insights did they trigger? How has a particular incident moved you, reshaped your attitudes and values?"

ORGANISATION AND EXPRESSION

Strengths

You write well. The personal experience you shared with the reader, although second-hand, was for the most part engaging.

Areas for Improvement

The entire introductory paragraph is extremely weak; just take a look at it and compare it with the conclusion (your final paragraph), in which you actually make your point. Delving further into your introduction: your first sentence, *One should be provided with ample opportunities*...it's not at all clear what you're getting at here — what do you mean by "should"?

Suggestions

If you wish to write a reflective essay, you need to make sure you fully understand the purpose of that format. And, likewise, you must understand the argumentative format as well. These two format have been chosen by the authors of "The Guru Method" specifically to aid you in those difficult moments when you are facing an exam and have a very short time to write a convincing piece of writing. The idea behind the choice of those 2 formats is:

(1) Each offers an opportunity to showcase your intellectual capacity:

(2) Each provides a structured template to practise, so that you can avoid panic when you are sitting for the exam, and instead can feel confident because you have practiced writing both these types.

The one single promising way to improve your next essay:

After learning the formats of both the argumentative and reflective essay, study examples of both types that you can easily find on the Op-ed page of any major newspaper, and on the Internet.

ESSAY TOPICS: TOPIC TWO

TOPIC TWO

Consider the following comments and develop a piece of writing in response to one or more of them.

Your writing will be judged on the quality of your response to the theme; how well you organise and present your point of view, and how effectively you express yourself.

You will not be judged on the views or attitudes you express.

* * * * * * *

Advertising is the principal reason why the business person has come to inherit the earth.

James R. Adams

You can tell the ideals of a nation by its advertisements.

Norman Douglas

Advertising is a racket...its constructive contribution to humanity is exactly minus zero.

F. Scott Fitzgerald

What you say in advertising is more important than how you say it.

David Ogilvy

Those who prefer their English sloppy have only themselves to thank if the advertisement writer uses his mastery of vocabulary and syntax to mislead their weak minds.

Dorothy L. Sayers

ESSAYS AND ANALYSES: TOPIC ONE

ESSAY ONE

It has been quoted that "advertising is a racket...its constructive contribution to humanity is exactly minus zero". I can appreciate the negative suggestion of this quote that advertising can be irritating; and generally serves the purpose of drumming-up business for selfish purposes rather than the benefit of humanity. However, it is not the art of advertising itself which fails to serve humanity, but what purpose and motive this medium is utilised for. Advertising has in fact been employed by many companies and organisations in order to gain support to contribute positively and significantly to humanity.

Many non-government organisations (NGOs) use media advertising campaigns in order to gain financial and human support to make a difference to less fortunate communities. An example is an NGO called surf-aid that was established by a New Zealand doctor named Dave Jenkins. He once took a holiday to go surfing at a world-renowned group of islands in Indonesia called the Mentawais. During his trip he noticed the horrific suffering of the local inhabitants. The death rate from preventable diseases such as malaria, as well as malnutrition and natural disasters was harrowing. This sparked him to leave his highly-paid job in Singapore to establish surf-aid. Advertising was employed in the form of newspaper and magazine articles, as well as websites, facebook and twitter to attract financial and human support. The donations gained through advertising have led to a significant difference in this community as education and resources such as mosquito nets, clean water, sustainable food sources and emergency management supplies have been provided. This has led to a substantial reduction in deaths from malnutrition, malaria and natural disasters, which was made possible through advertising.

Other organisations such as the cancer society advertise to contribute to humanity in New Zealand. Each year the cancer society advertise the national daffodil day through mass media including television and radio adverts, billboards, websites, flyers, and street collectors. When people donate to the cause, they receive an artificial daffodil that can be pinned onto clothing. Funds that are collected through such advertising go towards assisting individuals with cancer and their families, scientific research projects to find a cure, and education campaigns to prevent the development of cancer. All of these interventions are aimed at having a positive contribution for humanity, which would not be possible without the effective use of advertising.

Finally, advertising is used in circumstances when organisations simply wish to remind citizens of behaviours which generate health and therefore make a positive impact on humanity. There are numerous television and radio adverts sponsored by the Ministry of Health to educate and encourage people to eat at least five servings of fruit and vegetables each day, aim to get at least 30 minutes of exercise daily, and also to offer free quit-smoking support. Such advertising campaigns primarily aim to have a positive contribution to those living in society.

Advertising is a vehicle that can be employed by many people, companies and organisations for a myriad of purposes. It is well known that advertising can be irritating and is often used to benefit such parties without contributing to humanity in any way. However, advertising can also be used by companies in a manner which aims to positively influence humankind. Many organisations such as surf-aid, the cancer society and the ministry of health have used advertising to gain support in order to effectively contribute to humanity. Advertising therefore is neutral, can be used for or against humanity, and should not be blamed for being a racket which does not help others.

THOUGHT AND CONTENT

Strengths
Your thesis is stated early on, and the line of thought developed from it is clear and coherent, making for a quick, smooth read.

Areas for Improvement
All three of your paragraphs in the body of the essay—those essential paragraphs intended to provide supportive examples for your thesis—deal exclusively with non-profit entities that utilize advertising. In sticking to this narrow focus, you fail to follow through on your promise, so to speak, of letting the reader know the positive contribution to humanity made by advertising utiliised by *companies*. You made that "promise" in the all-important introductory paragraph, when you wrote: *Advertising has in fact been employed by many companies and organisations.*

And you didn't stop there, but again referred to *companies* in the conclusion, devoting an entire sentence to the concept: *However, advertising can also be used by companies in a manner which aims to positively influence humankind.*

The reason why this is an "area for improvement" is not just because the reader is disappointed by your failure to address *companies*, but because when one addresses the general topic of "advertising," one is talking about a gigantic worldwide industry, in which for-profit entities are clearly the major players, yet you do not include them in your supportive examples at all.

Suggestions

The essay could have been greatly enhanced by the inclusion of positive contributions made not only by some companies, but by the advertising industry as a whole. That is, of course, if you agree that some of their activities do represent contributions to society.

Here are a few suggestions about such contributions you might have recognized (or might have argued that although they pretend to be serving humanity, they are not really contributing at all, depending on your view):

(1) Many of the world's largest business enterprises routinely generate "public service" advertisements aimed at raising awareness of such things as global warming and the consequent need for developing sustainable energy sources —

or the growing concerns about depletion of various natural resources.

(2) The advertising industry as a whole serves as a leading light in the art world, responsible for inspiring many new developments in audio and visual applications, and millions of jobs for people employed in worldwide marketing.

(3) Advertising dollars help finance huge events seen by billions of people all over the world, such as the upcoming FIFA World Cup in Brazil, events which contribute to an entire country's wealth in terms of tourism, etc.

ORGANISATION AND EXPRESSION

Strengths

The structural framework is well-crafted, which is what allows the essay to flow smoothly.

Areas for Improvement

Your second paragraph is overlong —no, that's too diplomatic— more accurately, your second paragraph can be said to be a monster, presenting a formidable challenge to the reader. If you divide that paragraph at a logical point, such as at the sentence beginning *Advertising was employed....*you will see that you actually wrote six

paragraphs, which would not be a problem if all 6 paragraphs were without flaw.

The much more serious problem is that it the overlong paragraph is a symptom of a lack of proper planning and organisation on the part of the essayist.

Suggestions

In future essay attempts, you need to have a very clear idea of which of the many details that come into your mind you actually need, and which details, not matter how engaging, must be left out because they do not contribute directly to your thesis. For example, although the story about Dave Jenkins is certainly interesting, you took time and space in the telling of it that might have been spent in more essential ways—in this case, it could have been spent both in better planning before the writing, and/or in going over your essay to look for errors and discrepancies after the writing is completed.

Although there is no strict requirement regarding length of the piece in writing these practice essays or the essay you will be writing for the Gamsat, it seems evident that either you did not time yourself when you wrote this essay, or that if you did time yourself, you yielded to the temptation to write much more than you had time for, and that was apparently the reason behind the weaknesses pointed out in the "Areas for Improvement" portions of this analysis.

The one single promising way to improve your next essay:

Planning: Before writing one word, devote at least 5 minutes to this important stage: First deciding on your thesis statement, then outlining what the content of each paragraph will be. And — this is quite essential: you must allot a few minutes for a final read-through when the essay is completed, to catch errors, etc. You may end up with a shorter essay, but remember, you're not going to be judged on length, you're going to be judged on quality of thought.

ESSAY TWO

Advertisement and marketing is everywhere in todays society. It is inescapable. From tv advertisements to stickers vandalised onto trains. The issue is where would we be without it, at what point does it become wrong and who is controlling the industry? I dont mean to say all advertisement is evil. Some in fact help us by letting us know of new and exciting opportunities or products. But this is the way these products have been framed. So then what do we believe? And how should and could this be regulated given that it is a world comprised of manipulation and persuasion of our needs, wants and in some cases ideals?

Advertisement is a part of our society. It is known fact that people who have marketed well have become successful. Like those countless machines that help 'tone up your abdominal muscles'. The product itself is weak but through advertisement they have made a lot of money. It is a vital part to success and in a sense is a major contributing factor to why the business man has taken over the world. But it is not the sole reason. The product that is being sold must have quality and affordability. Those two characteristics can be measured in numerous ways. But the bottom line is that if someone has a product that is too expensive or of lesser quality, the overall longevity of the business will be poor and ultimately will fail. Marketing is essential, but a quality and affordable product is the key.

As mentioned, marketing is an essential part of todays world. Through marketing we find out about new opportunities or products. It is when marketing becomes deliberately deceitful does it present a problem. The use of confusing language designed to mislead the common individual. It could be said that because a persons inability to understand the language they have only themselves to blame for their own deception or lack of comprehension. But is that fair? Should a person be targeted and, in a way, punished for not being ably to attend a private school as a child? There are laws to prohibit such underhanded tactics. But they assume that all people will understand the language. Or at least I hope so as the other option to prejudice is that they are deliberately letting marketing companies get away with strategies, such as this, to mislead us.

Elected officials are placed into power for the purpose of control. These positions exist to represent and protect the people. To represent a nation and it's ideals. So in a round a bout way you can gain insight into a nations ideals from its laws. But only an insight. Further more it could be said that through advertisement we can see the confines of the industry and therefore the laws surrounding that industry. So by extension of that we could say that through advertisement we can gain an insight into a nations ideals. In the case of laws and regulations prohibiting marketing companies should we have tougher ones? This is question that can only be answered by the people and not one person. Be it me or a elected official.

As of this point in time, I do not believe that the tactics and strategies being used by large marketing firms is being regulated strictly enough. Clever and manipulative, advertisement will always be around but it is up to the government to make sure that it does not cross a line into cohesion or cause inequality.

THOUGHT AND CONTENT

Strengths

What is clear is that you put a lot of thought into trying to come up with an approach to the general topic of advertising.

Areas for Improvement

It appears that you've overdone the thinking part, coming up with a plethora of ideas on various aspects of your chosen topic. Thus, you apparently ended up by being overcome with the weight of all these various, disorganized ideas and paid little or no attention to whittling down those thoughts to anything approaching a manageable idea for the single subject of an essay.

The basis for this guess about what might have happened to you is that the essay wanders. Even after reading this piece several times, it is difficult to grasp what you're talking about and what your main point is.

Thus the main area for improvement in the "Thought and Content" section of this analysis lies in your failure to provide even a minimal effort at a basic framing of the issue you chose to discuss. You wrote a piece of writing that "explored" the issues that you identified in your introductory paragraph. Those issues were expressed as numerous rhetorical questions that you apparently intended to answer by means of the paragraphs that follow. If that was indeed your intention, it did not work — no surprise there. It couldn't have worked; there was far too much material you wanted to cover.

SUGGESTIONS

(1) Adopt a new attitude in future, substituting the concept represented by the word "convince" for the word "explore" when formulating your objective for the writing of an essay. Consider the elements necessary for writing an argumentative essay, as succinctly outlined in "The Guru Method:" "An argumentative essay requires you to "…take a position, explain it and use reasons to consolidate it." If you had planned your essay with these objectives in mind, your position on the issue of advertising would've been stated at the outset, whereas in your piece of writing it is not even mentioned until the conclusion, and even then, only half-heartedly, and ineffectually.

(2) Keep in mind that your essay mark will be heavily weighted by the "Thought and Content" portion (by as much as 75%), so narrowing down your thoughts is crucial.

ORGANISATION AND EXPRESSION

Strengths

You write well; there is no doubt that if you decide to turn that talent in the direction of writing an actual argumentative essay, you will do well.

Areas for Improvement

What was said above, in the "Thought and Content" portion of this analysis bears repeating here: The essay wanders. Even after reading this piece several times, it is difficult to grasp what you're talking about and what your main point is.

Suggestions

(1) In an earlier analysis done for you, it was suggested that you follow the traditional 5-paragraph format for an argumentative essay. This suggestion was accompanied by an outline of what should be in each of those paragraphs; however, in this present submission, it seems the only part of that suggestion you followed was that you did, indeed, have 5

paragraphs. So, let's try an even simpler, easier description of what goes into the planning for an argumentative essay:

Step 1: What is my position, my claim? OK, I've got that -- now put it into a thesis statement. Step 2. OK, now I've got a sentence saying what I think. Why do I think that? Step 3: List of Reasons - 1. Reason 2. (Maybe even Reason 3). Step 4: Each one of those reasons gets a separate paragraph stating the reason, followed by an example to explain and support that single reason. Step 5: After that, the conclusion is easy.

(2) Since you were able to synthesize your thoughts into a clearly stated point of view in the concluding paragraph of the piece, why not take a lesson from that:

In your planning stage, , start with the plan for your conclusion (the concluding paragraph), and make sure that the ideas in it are what you want the reader to be thinking about when he's finished reading. You can then use that idea to help you formulate your thesis, which is usually introduced in the first paragraph. Lastly, then, work out the supportive examples.

The one single promising way to improve your next essay:

Formulate a thesis, introduce it at the outset, and stick to it like glue all the way.

ESSAY THREE

> Advertising is a racket...its constructive contribution to
> humanity is exactly minus zero.
>
> F. Scott Fitzgerald

Advertising has long been scored as the bane of television and radio, but its nature and content contributes to humanity by providing opportunity, not only for the little-known charity or the budding innovator, but also for the layperson in daily life.

Advertising provides an outlet for which charities, such as World Vision or the RSPCA, may explain their objectives to the wider community. Before I came across a poster at a bus stand, I was unaware that the Smith family offered child sponsorship. How many people may be willing to sponsor or contribute to these benevolent causes but are unaware of the means through which they may do so? Word of mouth is often insufficient for charities as these organisations are rarely the subject of conversation and as such, charities rely on advertising to promote their cause in the face of a broken world.

The livelihood of humanity revolves around a healthy economy. Without advertising, departmental store would have no way of promoting their goods. A subsequent collapse would see the redundancy of many workers. Within a field which is accountable for so many livelihoods, this would be catastrophic. Similarly, the young and aspiring innovator requires a pedestal on which he may place his ideas to have an opportunity to reap what he has sown in his hours of labour. Advertising promotes a vigorous economy.

However, the fruits of advertising are not limited to businesspeople. Aside from the obvious benefit that individuals glean from specials, they are informed of in the commercial industry, individuals are given an opportunity to relax and unwind. The commercials on television are wifely known as 'toilet break' times and many a witty commercial has found its way into a conversation between good friends. The leisurely nature of commercials serves humankind in general by providing another aspect of life that is not to be taken too seriously, but enjoyed.

Thus, while advertising is sometimes seen as burdensome, it gives many businesses and individuals the opportunity to thrive in the contemporary world. Not only does it promote the economy, it helps to provide a buffer against the rough tides of the rat race in which we live. The benefits of advertising are well known to many and its contribution to humanity widespread.

THOUGHT AND CONTENT

Strengths

Your line of thought is, for the most part, straightforward, cogent, and coherent.

Areas for Improvement

Noting that the above remark does include the phrase "for the most part," you may well ask what the exception is, and this is it: getting at the central essence of what you're trying to say is a bit difficult, because of the lack of consistency between the content of the thesis and that of the supportive examples in the three paragraphs that form the main body of the essay.

The thesis mentions the positive aspects of advertising as *providing opportunity, not only for the little-known charity or the budding innovator, but also for the layperson in daily life,* and although these are indeed eventually covered, one aspect of what eventually turns out to be a significant part of your thought content is not even given a nod in the introduction. The reader learns of it only at the outset of the 3rd paragraph, with this resounding topic sentence: *The livelihood of humanity revolves around a healthy economy.*

Suggestions

Pay greater attention in the planning stage to the thought and content of the introductory paragraph, as suggested in the "The Guru Method," guidebook for this practice course: "….if you have brainstormed well and chosen your guiding principles and key concepts well, it should practically write itself."

ORGANISATION AND EXPRESSION

Strengths

You're going in the right direction, in that this essay attempt represents an improvement over the organisation and expression of your earlier submission.

Also, the inclusion of your own experience in the example about charity advertising: *Before I came across a poster at a bus stand, I was unaware that…*enhanced the essay by injecting a human touch.

Areas for Improvement

Overall, the impact of the basically sound line of thought of the essay is marred by the carelessness seen in its composition—errors either of syntax or simple typos, which, although minor, serve to bring the reader to a halt each time one is encountered. If this happens only once, in an entire essay, it could go unremarked. However, the frequency of these small "bumps" effectively interrupts the "smooth flow" you should be aiming at. Here are just two examples of such errors:

(1) In the very first sentence of the essay, where obviously your best effort should be made, you have the word "scored," which stops the reader in his/her tracks, thinking of what you might have intended….did you mean "scorned?"

(2) Syntax: There is an abrupt, no doubt unintentional change of meaning within a single sentence that once again stops the reader: *The commercials on television are wifely known as 'toilet break' times and many a witty commercial has found its way into a conversation between good friends.*

The confusion is generated by the fact that the phrase "toilet break times," in addition to referring to the possibility of a break to attend to physical needs, usually connotes total dislike of commercials and therefore, when one is on air is an ideal time to get away from a thing one dislikes so intensely. In your sentence, however, this commonly understood concept is immediately followed in the very same sentence by a statement that has an opposite meaning —lauding commercials for their sometimes high entertainment value.

Moreover, the word *wifely* doesn't help at all; it stops the reader right at that point, wondering, again, what you could possibly have meant.

Suggestions

In spite of the improvement in organisation expression noted under "Strengths,"

above, the mark for this essay still does not rise above average. Note, however, that in all of the above critique, your conclusion has not been mentioned; this is because it's a positive element—one of the strongest elements in the piece.

Keep in mind that although you have been advised in both this analysis and the previous one to work on your introductory material, the conclusion is just as important. That's because, if properly written, the conclusion will leave the reader focused exactly on whatever thought you want him/her to be thinking when he's done. The suggestion here is that you build on your demonstrated ability to create a conclusion, and do the following:

Start the planning phase with your conclusion! Synthesize all the thoughts that, hopefully, have just come swirling wildly into your head into one or two sentences that contain the gist of what you want the reader to be thinking about when he or she has finished reading the essay. This will guide you in choosing the material both for the introduction and the supporting paragraphs.

In this instance, if you had written your conclusion first, you would have had this strong phrasing to guide you:

…while advertising is sometimes seen as burdensome, it gives many businesses and individuals the opportunity to thrive in the contemporary world. Not only does it promote the economy……

The one single promising way to improve your next essay:

Training yourself is the key. Think of getting a good mark the essay portion of the big cxam you plan to take as if it were a contest involving physical agility instead of mental prowess. What you would need inn order to prowess is plenty of practice. Professional athletes spend many hours in training each day, even after they've achieved top rank.

So, it's the same for mental prowess: what you need to do is writing training. Set yourself a goal to write, perhaps one essay every few days. First, you would select some quotes— make a list of quotes you find on the Web. Then, let some time go by, several days, so you don't have those quotes in mind; you barely even remember them. Now, set aside a time, set a timer, and go at it. 30 minutes only. Same conditions as at the Gamsat. Then, leave it; come back to it a day later, and try to approach the reading as if you were a marker for the test. Later, try the same exercise again, trying to avoid making the same kind of errors you found in the first effort.

If you repeat this process for a few weeks, you should notice considerable improvement.

ESSAY FOUR

"Advertising is a racket its constructive contribution to
humanity is exactly minus zero"

James R. Adams

Never has such a statement been so distorted. "<u>Advertising</u>" is a way of persuasive communication to "<u>humanity</u>" us the people. Advertising has evolved into a vastly complex form of communication shaping many things associated with humanity, ranging from religion to smoking, even what we have for breakfast. Advertising draws humanity in by many misleading and promising adverts. But have we gone too far over the last few decades? With many controversial and inappropriate advertisements banned for being too inappropriate for viewers. I think that all adverts contribute to humanity in two ways; 1) a positive way and 2) a negative way.

"<u>Contribution to humanity Is exactly minus zero</u>" by this quote James R. Adams suggests that advertising has no effect on humanity what so ever. I strongly disagree with this statement. Advertising has had a strong positive contribution to humanity. One example of this is portrayed by the images advertised on cigarette packages. The images depict the damage smoking can cause to your health and include images of diseased organs and human suffering. Smoking kills up to half of its users and nearly 6million people each year, what's more shocking is that 600,000 of these deaths are a result of non-smokers being exposed to second-hand smoke. Urgent action must be taken otherwise the annual death toll could rise to more than 8 million by 2030, the notion of this is extremely terrifying. In 2012 there was a paper published in the American journal of preventative medicine about the effects of these images on smokers. The study found that the graphical pictures present on cigarette packages greatly reduce the number of children who begin smoking and increased the number of smokers who quit. In addition graphic warnings can persuade smokers to protect the health of non-smokers by smoking less inside the home and avoiding smoking near children. Studies carried out after the implementation of pictorial package warnings in Brazil, Canada, Singapore and Thailand consistently show that pictorial warnings significantly increase people's awareness of the harms of smoking. Evidently images advertised on cigarette packages have had a huge contribution to humanity. The continued use of these images on smoking packets will continue to decrease the number of smokers who quit and spread awareness to smokers to protect the health of non-smokers by not smoking inside.

In contrast advertising can have a negative impact on society. Prohibition of inappropriate advertisements has happened many times. Many adverts have been prohibited from TV due to various reasons including nudity, sex scenes, violence, depicting suicide bombers to name a few. An example of an inappropriate advert was the Xbox 360's shooting advert, where Commuters on a tube platform play an imaginary game of "Shoot 'em Up" with their fingers. This advert was banned as it was judged as being too violent and portraying the use of handguns. With Nine-Thousand murders in 2010 being associated with handguns in the United statent videos has been associated with children developing a violent nature in there later life' it whilst spreades, this type of advertising is the last thing that the public need to see. Watching violent videos has been associated with children developing a violent nature in there later life's. Therefore advertising can also affect humanity in a negative way.

Particular adverts should be banned at particular times of the day. For example gambling, smoking and alcohol adverts should be banned during sports broadcasts, as these adverts are influencing humanity in a negative way. Exposure to these adverts could be risk factors for the development of gambling, smoking and alcohol problems in the future. Similarly banning adverts that include sexual references and drugs during times of the day when children's shows are on should also be stopped, as these images are highly graphic and inappropriate for young children and could potentially result in "adultification" of children. In addition banning many inappropriate adverts on billboards and bus stations should be actioned. Billboards dominate public space with hyper-sexualised messages, buses are painted with semi-naked women. Children are absorbing these distorted messages about their bodies, sexuality and gender roles because the advertising Standards Board does not consider objectification of women contrary to prohibitions on discrimination and vilification. These are highly sexualised adverts that target children, and the advertising industry is getting away with it," Dr Hambleton said. "There is strong evidence that premature sexualisation is likely to be detrimental to child health and development, particularly in the areas of body image and sexual health.' Thus advertising can have a huge negative impact on society particularly young innocent children.

In conclusion advertising has and will continue to contribute to humanity in a negative and positive way. There will always be controversial and inappropriate advertising some will escape and reach the public and some will be stopped along the way. Regardless advertising will continue to evolve, and will always be around "Advertising has existed as far back as 3000 BC". Advertising is ubiquitous, appearing everywhere you looked, listened, moved, called, read, drove, flew, worked, and played. Buy this! Buy that! Free sample! Call us! Email us! Visit us! Follow us!

THOUGHT AND CONTENT

Strengths

Your line of thought is clear and coherent.

Areas for Improvement

A major area for improvement the lack of a well-chosen thesis that narrows down a broad topic to a manageable focus. As you know, you will be asked to write an essay as part of the Gamsat because that is the recommended format for effectively displaying your power of intellect. In the argumentative essay, the writer emphatically takes one side of an issue, as opposed to what you've done here. By setting forth a thesis that says: *I think that all adverts contribute to humanity in two ways; 1) a positive way and 2) a negative way*, the only position you've actually taken is a position "on the fence."

As in your earlier submission, you have once again, apparently unwittingly, ended up with a relatively non-controversial thesis statement that says, in effect, "It isn't a minus zero, advertising isn't all bad—there are two sides, and I'm going to write about both of them. And furthermore, I'm not going to say whether I favor either side over the other." Thus, although this time around you've indicated there are two sides, by not taking one of those sides and strongly defending it, you've come out sounding indecisive and ineffectual.

Perhaps this was a result of a misunderstanding of the portion of the earlier analysis done for yu, which mentioned it's much easier to develop a strong convincing argument if the issue you're going to write about is controversial enough that there are two sides. That was not meant to imply in any way that you should take it upon yourself to discuss both sides. However, that is what you chose to do here, and the effect was to greatly weaken the essay.

Suggestions

Understand that when one takes a position and gives only the positive points about the issue to try and convince the reader of the validity of his or her way of thinking, that doesn't imply that the other side has no positive points—what is implied is that you've considered both sides and decided that the positive points of the one you've chosen greatly outweigh those of the other side.

Suggestion 1: When you're in the planning stage of your next argumentative essay, approach it as you would a job interview: there, you want to convince the person across the desk that you possess the exact skills and traits he or she is looking for. Sure, you've got some negative traits as well, but would you feel compelled to mention them, too?

(Some advice books for job-seekers go so far as to provide sample responses so you won't be caught off-guard in case the interviewer asks you, "What would you say is your greatest fault?" In case you're curious, a typical response of this sort would be: "I tend to overwork a bit, staying in the office after hours to make sure everything is completed properly."}

Suggestion 2: It may also be helpful if you consider the difference between essay writing and report writing. Traditionally, media news reporters strive to be objective in their reporting, giving both sides of an issue and keeping their own opinions completely out of the picture.

However, if that same journalist writes an editorial (also known as an "opinion piece") about an issue that he's done a lot of reporting on, he is then free to "editorialize." Therefore, the suggestion for you is that you might like to take a look at a few editorials on the Op-Ed page of any newspaper in the English-speaking world. All the respected ones are online; their editorials are good examples of what is, in effect, a contemporary well-written essay.

ORGANISATION AND EXPRESSION

Strengths

There was a modest improvement in your choice of objective examples, rather than just your own opinions to support your position were, in

Areas for Improvement

The introductory paragraph is not focused, providing a lot of unneeded information that does not directly lead the reader to a complete understanding of what your main point is going to be. For instance, what's your question *have we gone too far over the last few decades?* got to do with anything you present later on?

Your two paragraphs about the negative impact of advertising, taken together, are weaker than the one about the images on cigarette packages (that paragraph is overlong, and can be considered the equivalent of two paragraphs, in any case). The reason why the images one is stronger is that in it you have provided objective, credible evidence to support your view that this type of advertising is actually effective in achieving the results it was aiming for. The paragraphs on negative effect, however, give no solid evidence of the effect on humanity, which was supposed to be the point; rather, you drift into a long series of opinion-based statements, with one brief stab at credibility, quoting a "Dr. Hambleton" about whom you provide no credentials, and who is only expressing his or her own opinion.

Suggestions

(1) Suggestion: You could have cut those entire two paragraphs on the negative effect, and focused on the positive effect as a thesis, but only if you had given more than one example of that: do you see that, in trying to take on so much, you gave short shrift to the positive effects by writing exclusively about cigarette packets? Of course, if the images idea was the only positive point about advertising you could think of to use as an example—and you didn't want to choose to argue exclusively about the negative points because you couldn't provide any solid credible evidence of the damage those adverts do to humanity—then perhaps it would have been better to choose a different topic altogether to write about.

(2) Suggestion: write clearly <u>in your own words and your own style.</u>

Your first sentence mars the essay right at the very crucial outset. Even if the marker employed by Gamsat to read your essay may not know that *Never has such a statement been so distorted* is the first sentence of a sample essay on   Page 25 of <u>The Guru Method,</u> that particular sentence in the context of your essay is entirely misplaced, and is likely not to be understood by the marker or anyone else.

That sentence, in that sample essay, referred to the distortion of a well-known sentence by reformulating it: thus, the old saying, "Money is the root of all evil," was reformulated by the author of the quote into "The love of money is the root of all evil." Regarding the quote you chose, there was no such distortion of any statement of any kind.

(3) Suggestion: If you're going to identify the quote you selected as the stimulus for your essay, it's a really good idea to get your facts right. The fact that you attributed the quote about advertising being a racket to someone named Adams, when it was actually by F. Scott Fitzgerald, gives an impression right off the bat that you are careless.

The one single promising way to improve your next essay:

Write your next essay under the same conditions that you will be subjected to when you take the Gamsat -- that is, with no ability to consult any notes or do any research, and keeping to the strict time limit of 30 minutes—which should include at least 5 minutes for planning and organising before any attempt is made to write one word, and a few minutes at the end of the allotted time for you to go over your work to make quick corrections that might make a big difference—such as cutting an overlong paragraph into two paragraphs..

ESSAY FIVE

What one says in advertising is not more important than how one says it. The content of advertising will go unnoticed if it is not delivered in an effective way. Conversely, if an advertisement is eye-catching and memorable, even a misled idea can be widely received by the audience. There are certain issues which are important regardless of the way they are presented, but generally advertisements are ineffective if not delivered well.

How one says something is very important in advertising. This can allow the most boring issue to become interesting and noticed. A recent advertisement on television aims to sell vitamin D tablets to women of all ages. This uninteresting idea to many women is presented with fluoro skeletons dancing. This is eye catching and demonstrates bone strength. Smart conveyance of ideas that may seem unimportant to the public can result in successful advertisement of a product.

Even a contentious or potentially misled issue can be presented in a way that catches the attention of the public and initiates debate. A current television advertisement about a sports bra that is supposed to reduce the amount breasts move during exercise has caused debate. Many women in the public feel that the add is not realistic because it demonstrates women with smaller than average breasts. Although the advertisement was intended to sell a product, the way it was presented, with women bouncing on gym balls, is eye-catching and has gained much attention.

Very important issues are able to be widely received by the audience regardless of the way they are presented. Political advertisements in the lead up to an election are traditionally serious and repetitive. The way they are presented does not matter to the audience. Those that create these advertisements do not try to make them too fancy but rather get straight to the point, because they are more concerned the entire message is clearly presented than in doing something fun or unique.

How the message is delivered is much more important than the content of the message in advertising. When delivered in an effective way, even content about boring issues can be noticed. Political advertisements are an example of advertising that gets the message across regardless of how seriously it is presented. To successfully advertise and entice the audience into buying their product or agreeing with their opinion, the way the message is delivered is paramount.

THOUGHT AND CONTENT

Strengths

Your decision to select a single aspect of an integral part of our contemporary society, and take a position on it, is a good start on the path toward writing a cogent argumentative essay.

Areas for Improvement

The essay is flawed by two major weaknesses:

(1) Your thesis, which appears to be stated in the introductory paragraph, suffers from the absence of a clear definition of a term that just happens to be a key word. The word in question is "effective," which was used in each of two iterations of your main point within the introductory paragraph:

First, this wording: *The content of advertising will go unnoticed if it is not delivered in an effective way.* and later: *but generally advertisements are ineffective if not delivered well.*

The problem is that you fail to define the word "effective," so the reader is left to assume, from the general tenor of your argument throughout the remainder of the piece, that you consider an ad to be effective if it receives attention. This is nothing if not surprising, because — at least in commercial advertising — the criterion for determining whether any advertising is "effective" is traditionally not the attention it draws, but rather the bottom line: whether whatever is being advertised ultimately brings in revenue.

Although you indeed appear to acknowledge that the goal of most commercial advertising is to sell a product or service, you do not even so much as mention whether the examples of "successful" advertising that you present in the body of the essay ever in fact increased sales of the product or service they were promoting. All you are concerned about is whether people paid attention to them.

(2) See the "Organisation and Expression" section, below, for a discussion of the second major weakness of the essay.

Suggestions

For the purpose of this course, and the Gamsat, it would be very wise to choose a subject about which you know a good deal, and about which you can write a reasoned essay that shows depth of thought. This advice is offered because this essay submission leaves the impression that you are not particularly well-informed about the details of how the field of advertising works.

ORGANISATION AND EXPRESSION

Strengths

Your mastery of English, in terms of vocabulary, sentence structure, grammar, etc., is evident, and will serve you well in future essay attempts.

Areas for Improvement

The claims you offered to substantiate your thesis are insufficient to be convincing,

because those statements are generalizations that offer no specific evidence to back up what you are saying. For example, even if you had provided a definition of "effective" which tells the reader that for the purposes of this essay, "effective" advertising is that which gains attention, you haven't provided any way of quantifying that attention. You say ....*is eye-catching and has gained much attention.* How much is *much attention?* Did you mean that among your circle of friends and acquaintances, the ad is quite popular, or...what?

Suggestions

With regard to the question of "how much?"" above. Again, knowing your subject well would have helped. With some subject matter, it is difficult to provide statistical evidence to back up claims when writing an argumentative essay, but in the case of advertising, it's quite easy, since the subject is quantifiable, and there is plenty of data gained through polling and actual devices connected to people's TV's to gauge their viewing preferences.

Another suggestion: avoid the frequent repetition of the same thought that characterizes this piece.

The one single promising way to improve your next essay:

During the planning phase of your next argumentative essay, before starting to write, imagine the person who is going to read and mark the essay. Have a little imaginary conversation with him/her, in which you not only make statements, but that person answers. For example, you might say, "Most people are not concerned about what actions their government takes; they're too busy watching TV." Your eventual reader of your essay answers, "Oh, really? How do you know that?" This is the kind of question the reader of this submission asks when he reads it: "How do you know this, and how do you know that?" "Who says so?"

ESSAY SIX

"What you say in advertising is more important than how you say it" a famous quote by David Ogilvy and "You can tell the ideals of a nation by its advertisements" by Norman Douglas. These quotes given by famous personalities suggest different views of advertisements which has to be clearly analyzed and backed up with proper examples .

In retrospect of the ideas one company have or the product that it produces , an advertisement is something which gives away the propaganda of details of their production . It can also be considered as the awareness brought about by industries on their product for their benefit. If this is the definition that we choose for advertisements we must be making advertisements as excellent as possible which would lead to David's conclusion on advertisements.Else if advertisements were considered to be the circumspect of the situations and products that a company produces and a clear cut view of the intentions of company then the group of advertisements in a nation will surely point towards the ideals of the nation , which is the definition given by Norman Douglas.

On analyzing both of these statements one could find the first one more prevalent as more or less the major share of the advertisements rely on the way of introduction with the glamour of the actor or actress with staggering lines of scripts introduced and mindboggling styles which will surely influence the viewer . The more they see about the advertisement one would easily gets glued on to the fact of result and impact that it produces rather than the way in which it produces the desired result. The examples of advertisements starting from cooldrinks that clearly portrays the cacophony of the situations and the unprecedented action , which draws attention of any viewer satisfies the need of the drinks in daily situations and also creating the mood generality through which the scenario agree with your surroundings forcing you to do the same which is influential. This would lead to the most legible conclusion that it's the way of the advertisements that matters the most and the content of the product is of lesser importance .

On this ever changing planet government has been promoting advertisements from all and also self introducing advertisements regarding various awareness programs and decisions . The viewer can seriously be influenced by these various matters which is really juggernaut to crack . As considering David's conclusion regarding advertisements we could see that the advertisements always try to create a vague understanding of the product so if the nations advertisements are like this , no matter who makes it all it will always be like looking through a smeared glass where you cannot see the other side clearly while you have the vision and beauty of the outside views ,always unclear , packaged in the golden melody without revealing the threshold of chaos and unworthiness the product or theme in the advertisement which was shown.

Thought and Content

Strengths

Although trying to manage writing about 2 different quotes is not advisable for a person who is inexperienced in essay-writing, the very fact that you did try to take on such a large chunk of work to be completed within a very limited time does indicate you are ambitious. This may also mean that it's likely you'll be able, in the future, to come up with a cogent thesis and coherent line of thought.

Areas for Improvement

The main area for improvement in the "Thought and Content" section of this essay analysis is also the major flaw of the entire piece: it's the fact that you failed to present any thesis. You have, instead, presented an "analysis" of the issue of advertising –– indeed, you use the word: "analyze" in your introductory paragraph, quoted here: *These quotes given by famous personalities suggest different views of advertisements which has to be clearly analyzed and backed up with proper examples…*

It is very important that you learn the distinction between the use of the word "analysis" in this document you are reading now, (which is titled "Essay Analysis)" and the word "analyze" as you used it in your introductory paragraph. The definition of the verb "analyze" is to examine some information in detail for purposes of explanation and interpretation – and that is what you would expect the person writing this essay analysis to do.

However, you, in writing your practice essays, and for the Gamsat test itself, are not expected to analyze and explain;   rather, you are expected to create a piece of writing that achieves the overall purpose of an essay, and which is outlined succinctly in your study guide, "The Guru Method." Among its guidelines you will find this important basic point: "An argumentative essay requires you to evaluate the validity of the quotation, take a position,......."

Suggestions

It is strongly suggested that in future, you substitute the concept represented by the word "convince" for the word "analyze" during the crucial minutes when you are planning an argumentative essay based on whatever quote you've just chosen. Perhaps you can understand this better if you consider the reason you are going to be required by the Gamsat to write an essay in the first place. The people considering your application for admission want to get some idea of your intellectual ability. Now, think about this: What do you think will showcase your intellectual ability more --- a piece of writing in which you make an effort to explain and interpret, and build upon, someone else's idea (which is what you tried to do) – or a piece of writing that shows what are clearly your own creative, original, thought-provoking, ideas?

Also, be aware that the quotes that are supplied are only intended as a stimulus to thought. Therefore, although you might find it useful to briefly explain what you believe the author of the quote was getting at, it is not necessary to do so; you could, if you wish, just write something about advertising that does not necessarily relate to what the author said at all.

ORGANISATION AND EXPRESSION

Strengths

Your knowledge of English is sufficient that, if you try to organise your essay in simpler language and shorter sentence that come to the point, you will be well on the way to writing a comprehensible piece of work.

Areas for Improvement

The essay is not well-organised, making it very hard for the reader to identify and follow your train of thought; moreover, your style of writing features excessively long, wandering sentences, and this contributes to the feeling of confusion the reader gets when trying to uncover your meaning.

Suggestions

Strive for greater simplicity:

The organisation of an essay: your structure should enable you to make your thesis clear in the introductory paragraph; and the following paragraphs should contain "proper examples" such as you referred to in your first paragraph. Here's what an argumentative essay really is: In it, you are saying to the reader:

(1) This is what I think -- (introductory paragraph: major theme, or thesis)

(2) Here's why I think so (3 or more supporting paragraphs with examples to prove your point)

(3) So, now you can see why I said what I did in the 1st paragraph (conclusion)

A suggestion of less importance than the above, but nevertheless something you should not forget, is that it is not acceptable, when quoting a famous person, to refer to him by his given name (unless you yourself happen to know him personally), such as you did here: *which would lead to David's conclusion*

The one single promising way to improve your next essay:

Familiarize yourself with the two formats -- the argumentative essay and the reflective essay – which are outlined in "The Guru Method." Focus especially on pages 6-23. These guidelines have been worked out specifically to aid you in those difficult moments when you are facing an exam and have a very short time to write a convincing piece of writing.

ESSAY SEVEN

In the industrialized world advertising has, with no doubt, become an essential tool that is vital to facilitate commercial dealings. "Be wise and advertise" has become the catch-call of successful merchandising that without it one's business is destined to fail. However, like any other tool, advertising is a double-edge weapon that serves to aware customers to the benefits of the advertised commodity, while at the same time, aiming at improving the prospects of profiting for the advertiser. The problem therefore lies when advertising is merely made to increase the profit of the advertiser without providing customers with what the advertisement promised them to provide. This poses an ethical issue that touches on the morale of advertising as a construct and the community that supports such practice.

Often than not we come across large banners and signs that show products entirely wrapped in a context that is appealing to the consumer yet doesn't necessary deliver what it promises. "Thirst quencher" was the recent fad proffered by Coca Cola Australia for the lemonade drink Solo that contains 6 spoon-full of sugar and a host of acidic solutions. Would that what anyone would drink when thirsty without risking diabetes or weight gain! At the global level advertisement has been made part of the states agenda. We have witnessed how Hollywood has been transformed into a governmental enterprise over the past 10 years. "3 heroes" featuring George

Clooney was filmed during the eve of the Iraqi war and soon after the miserable failure of the US government to show the slightest evidence of the so-called "weapons of man destruction" to the inspectors of the United Nations.

Unfortunately and quite alarmingly, advertising does not stop at that level of deception but transcends the psychology of the culture it strives within to create an illusion of "must-haves" by which advertisements provoke the consumer to have the possession of the advertised item not out of need but to achieve the "air" the advertisements elude the customer to create. An advertisement does not make it to the T.V. until it has had the approval of the advertising enterprises psychologists. "We consider ourselves successful when those who do not need our products buy them" said Thomas Dobos, an American executive and publicist.

This mass-production of psychologically tailored advertisements, large on promises small on delivery, stands as a proof to the failure of the mechanisms employed by such industry, and in turn the moral system of the society. If we are to claim honesty and to preserve the moral fabric of our society we should not support deception by buying falsely hallowed products. The recent move to show photographs of severely ill people and the different ailments smoking causes on cigarettes packet has been a victory for honest advertising the benefit of which practice will be the consumer's. Only this way we can pride ourselves for making an honest living, it is when we advertise our merchandises for what they are.

Thought and Content

Strengths

Your thesis statement comes early on, and is clearly stated.

Areas for Improvement

Although, as noted above, your thesis is clearly stated in the introductory paragraph, trouble begins immediately thereafter. The problem is: the lack of relevance of the first example you provide as evidence to support your concern that: *The problem therefore lies when advertising is merely made to increase the profit of the advertiser without providing customers with what the advertisement promised them to provide.*

Instead of providing an example that is going to properly help the development of your line of thought, (a line of thought which is supposed to be based on your argument just quoted), you give an example that doesn't fit. While your objective here should be to give a sample of advertising that is clearly deceptive, instead, all you quote from the advertisement is a claim that the drink is a *Thirst quencher.* You don't go on to quote any claims about whether the drink is good for health or not, you just complain that it's a threat to health.

Since the question of whether any drink in the entire universe is actually a thirst quencher or not is entirely a matter of opinion, it is hard to see what's deceptive in this ad. The Solo ad, at least as far as the reader knows, never said the drink was healthy in the first place. (What's more, there's a nutrition label on it, as required by law, for all to see how much sugar and acidic solutions are in it, isn't there?) So, where's the deception?

The next example is the one about the global level, where you make the really provocative claim that *Hollywood has been transformed into a governmental enterprise over the past 10 years*. With a bombshell like that, you really need to provide an example that's a bit more convincing than a reference to a film that had George Clooney in it. An apparently obscure film which I not on any list of films that particular actor has appeared in, or directed, or wrote. Thus, your second example — which is very, very vague, given the severity of the claim it was meant to support — hardly qualifies as convincing evidence.

Suggestions

Limit your choice of topic to something you know comparatively well. If you knew the world of advertising a bit better, you probably would not have had much difficulty coming up with some pretty serious examples of truly deceptive advertising, such as, say, a few of the financial companies which in large part helped create the recent worldwide recession.

ORGANISATION AND EXPRESSION

Strengths

Your ability to write in a style that engages and holds the reader's attention is noteworthy.

Areas for Improvement

The entire 3rd paragraph seems to be the result of a lack of proper planning. It is an uncalled-for diversion from the thesis. Not only do you introduce an entirely new concept, but you provide no valid example, other than one man's statement. What's more, by abandoning the straight and narrow (your thesis) you apparently unknowingly wandered into a "mine field." Here's why: if it were not for the concept of "creating a need," the world would not have the benefit of modern technological development as we know it. That's because a surprisingly large number of new inventions have to be sold to a resistant public that does not understand the practical usefulness of the new thing, in other words, people think, "I've never needed anything like that before, and neither did my parents. What do I need it for?" So, the advertiser's job is to "create the need." Here's just one example: health workers trying to eliminate endemic diseases in underdeveloped regions of the world often have to figure out how to overcome resistance of the local population to vaccination. In other words, they have to "create the need" amongst that population.

One other reason why it was stated above that you entered a mine field: There is a very vexing question associated with your apparent idea that it is going to be perfectly clear to anybody whether there is a "need" for a certain product, and everyone ought to not buy that product. In a democratic society, who is going to make that determination whether there is a "need" for something, and then tell the public, "You don't need that." Of course, if you want to live in a place like Afghanistan as it was, and may be again, you can indeed have that decided for you: the Taliban decided, when they were in charge, that females don't need an education, and nobody at all needs art or music, or TV, or, basically, fun of any kind.

Suggestions

Here's an idea: In your planning phase, before you write one word, start with the conclusion — meaning, start with the main idea you want your reader to have when he's finished reading your essay.- Your conclusion in this essay has a kernel of thought that you could have developed into a more interesting and stimulating essay. After all, your target audience is hardly going to find it surprising that some advertising is deceptive, so why not make your central thesis the ideas you introduced in the conclusion as to how people might fight this

scourge of deceptive advertising, as you see it,-- this could include examples of what's been done already in various parts of the world in the way of legislation and punishment.

The one single promising way to improve your next essay:

Identify your argument with a clear thesis statement early, and then focus on it like a laser beam throughout the remainder of your piece,

ESSAY EIGHT

"Advertising is a racket and its constructive contribution to |humanity is exactly minus zero".

Scott F. Fitzgerald

In the late 1980's, companies moved their campaign ground from radio to television. It was a time when society was slowly getting accustomed to the words such as television and internet. In this essay we shall discuss how these campaigns didn't contribute to the betterment of the society but worked for the company's materialistic and financial gains. Advertising is such an intelligently built trap - a racket. Firstly we shall elaborate on how the market leaders influence the most vulnerable of the society, that is, children and young people. Secondly, we shall look into few classic examples of such advertising campaigns. To sum it up, we shall discuss about how these advertisements influence the innocent minds of our society and discuss few of the classic and contemporary examples to prove it.

First of all, let us talk about how these companies influence the children and the young minds of the day. Young people can be influenced quite easily. This weakness is what the advertising companies exploit. In very populous and developing countries like India and China, where seventy percent of the total population are under thirty to thirty five years old, such ad campaigns leave a lasting effect. This means that such campaigns are able to influence approximately twenty five percent of the world's population. Soft drink giants like Coca Cola Inc. and Pepsi Co. have a good market in such countries due to the influence they have on young minds as these people are more connected to most powerful media; they watch more television so they are more exposed to such ads which are presented on television. These young minds are knowingly giving into a product which doesn't have any nutritional value. These big companies use their favourite media personality or sportsmen to campaign for their products thus easily influencing these fragile minds.

Secondly, the ad campaigns by Dominos Pizza in the late 1990's are other classic examples. They used very creative ads to present a pizza as a healthy food. Recent studies have shown that a medium pizza provides a total energy of 9900KJ and it has very less nutritional value. Especially the ones sold by Dominos had very little nutritional value as the goal of these fast food chains are not about the betterment of the society but their own financial gain. They were ready to spend any amount of money to better their advertising campaigns to gain more market share. These companies prove over again that such ad campaigns do more bad to the community than good. We are left with more obese people in this world than we had had in the 1990's.

Studies have also proven how these soft drinks affect the human body. The chain of chemical reactions that these unknown recipes of soft drinks set off in our complex biological systems is unbelievable. These chemicals are making them more aggressive. Studies have also proven that long term consumption of these soft drinks creates cancer. These big corporates knowingly ingest such carcinogens for their mere financial gains.

The buying power of people in the developed countries like the U.S.A and Australia has had a linear increase from the 1990's and so has the influence of the big corporations. The pace of life has changed so much since the 1990's that people are easily influenced by such ad campaigns on television and on the internet, which propagate fast food and soft drinks. People give into it as they are so easily accessible. Today, Australia and the U.S.A are high up in the list of the most obese nations in the world. They are also high up in the list of countries plagued by different types of cancers.

All the aforesaid examples convey the same message – that these ad campaigns have had no constructive side to it. They contributed very less to the community. The recent studies are proving that they contributed negatively by influencing young minds, making them more aggressive and obese. The recent rise in the reported case of cancers in young people who live a fast paced life is also not a surprise. Big corporations like Coca Cola Inc., Pepsi Co. and Dominos have knowingly poisoned our minds and bodies for their materialistic intentions.

THOUGHT AND CONTENT

Strengths

Interpreting your chosen quote and developing your own thought-provoking

theory on the basis of that interpretation shows originality.

Areas for Improvement

Your aim in any argumentative essay is to present an argument that will convince the reader that your position on the specific subject you've chosen makes more sense than any opposing argument. This implies that the topic is controversial to begin with. Now, in your essay, your main point (your argument) is stated as follows: ...*these campaigns didn't contribute to the betterment of the society but worked for the company's materialistic and financial gains.* Are there two sides to this argument?

You seem to be expressing moral indignation about the situation you've presented in that leading sentence; apparently your own belief is that the proper role of advertising by major companies is to benefit society, and not to gain financial profit. But if that is indeed your position, it is a very unusual position, to say the least. How many people think, as you apparently do, that advertisers have a moral responsibility to society and should not have profit as their prime concern? If this is what you think, you should explain it and justify it, instead of simply complaining about companies using advertising in the same rather unsurprising ways that advertising has always been used—to profit the advertiser.

A further weakness with regard to the "thought and content" element of this essay is the vague quality of the evidence (the studies) you provide in support of your claim that advertising has actually caused the rise in obesity and some cancers. This is a bridge too far, because none of the studies you quote point to advertising as a <u>cause</u> of anything.

While these developments (growth in advertising and growth in obesity) were simultaneous, no one has claimed cause and effect; indeed, there are many other variables besides advertising that observers have pointed to as possible causes, including the rise in wealth that made possible the availability of abundant food choices, and the spread of labor-saving devices leading to a sedentary lifestyle.

Suggestions

Define your terms. While defining terms is certainly encouraged ordinarily – it is essential in any case such as this, where you are taking an unusual position. While it is certainly common for people to criticize corporate advertising and accuse it of earning huge profits at the expense of society, most critics accept the fact that in a capitalist economy, businesses are not set up to help society. Rather, they accept that the role of advertising is to increase profit for business— and it is the role of society to rise up, protest, demanding a curb to this kind of advertising if they recognize it as a harmful influence.

ORGANISATION AND EXPRESSION

Strengths

Your writing is clear and direct, and certainly conveys the strength of your own convictions.

Areas for Improvement

(1) Right at the outset, you make a glaring error of fact: *In the late 1980's, companies moved their campaign ground from radio to television. It was a time when society was slowly getting accustomed to the words such as television and internet.* The fact is that TV began replacing radio in the 1950's. While the person who marks your Gamsat essay may skim through some portions of it, you can count on him or her to read the first sentence, and this introductory sentence is doubly unfortunate.

Here's why: your first sentence isn't even necessary; the historical info about TV and the Internet is just tangential at best to your argument. In other words, even if you had the correct decade, this would not have been a good way to start the all-important first paragraph of your essay — but now that you did make that error in the very first sentence, you've introduced a suspicion in the mind of the reader that you are not well-informed, to say the least.

(2) Re: You note that the total time was 40 minutes. It's always a good idea to time yourself when you write practice essays; in this case, that information should have told you that the essay you wrote was too long, since you will only have 30 minutes total time when you sit for the Gamsat.

(3) The entire first paragraph was overly long; in creating the very short piece of writing that you will inevitably have to end up with because of the time constraint, you simply do not have time for the lengthy (and rather boring) introduction you wrote, which consists mostly of "First, I'll tell you about this, and then I'll tell you about that."

Suggestions

(1) Know your topic adequately. As in many other situations in the fast-paced lives we live today, you are only going to have the benefit of a few minutes' time from the person who marks your Gamsat essay, and therefore, in this case, the old adage that first impressions are important is especially relevant. That's why, during the planning stage, you need to make sure you know enough about the topic you select to write about it accurately.

(2) Regarding the 40 minute result on this essay: Once you had that result, It would have been more useful to you had you taken the trouble to try again, even a few times, timing yourself each time until you managed to produce an essay that contains all your thoughts within the required 30-minute time framework— and had then submitted that practice essay for review.

The one single promising way to improve your next essay:

Planning is the most important element that will improve your next essay. Plan carefully and thoroughly before putting anything down in writing, so that you can say what you want to say, convincingly, in a concise manner.

ESSAY TOPICS: TOPIC THREE

TOPIC TWO

Consider the following comments and develop a piece of writing in response to one or more of them.

Your writing will be judged on the quality of your response to the theme; how well you organise and present your point of view, and how effectively you express yourself.

You will not be judged on the views or attitudes you express.

* * * * * * *

Gluttony kills more than the sword.

Proverb

The first law of dietetics seems to be if it tastes good, its bad for you.

Isaac Asimov

Eating is touch carried to the bitter end.

Samuel Butler

To eat is human, to digest divine.

Charles T. Copeland

There is nothing to which men, while they have food and drink, cannot reconcile themselves.

George Santayana

ESSAYS AND ANALYSES: TOPIC THREE

ESSAY ONE

Gluttony kills more than the sword.

Christianity defines gluttony as one of the seven deadly sins. Therefore, an overconsumption of food, drink or money is obviously dangerous. Gluttony is essentially greed and when such greed overrides self-control, 'gluttony kills more than the sword'. This notion is evidenced in both modern and ancient worlds. Whilst the medieval glutton was charged with mortal sin for leading a lifestyle of excess, the contemporary glutton lies in a hospital bed having just suffered a heart attack. More subtle than the sword, gluttony kills and it does is so in greater numbers.

Gluttony was originally described in medieval theology, where it was associated with moral deformity, loss of control and the defiance of God. These charges in those times carried severe punishment. More specifically, those accused of being gluttonous were to be force-fed 'snakes, toads and rats in hell'. Moreover, individuals 'whose god was their belly' were considered incredibly selfish as their excessive desire for food and riches withheld from the needy. Gluttons were a low form of humanity and a blasphemous one at that. The overwhelming feature of a medieval glutton was an apparent lack of self-control characterized hoarding of food and subsequent defiance of God. We are told that war, poverty and starvation were rampant throughout history. During these dire times, gluttons overfed their own desires. This relentless overindulgence killed many others through forced starvation and abject poverty. The gluttons were not the peasants; they occupied the middle to upper class. Thus, whilst ancient conflicts may have killed many by sword, countless lives were lost to starvation – perhaps at the hands of the glutton.

Gluttony is pandemic in modern society. Today some of our biggest killers are cardiovascular disease and obesity. These ailments can be directly attributed to overconsumption. Both heart disease and obesity arise from excessive eating, and notably, a loss of self-control when it comes to food. More than murder, accidental death and suicide, these profoundly preventable conditions kill the most people in our society. Moreover, such diseases epitomize a loss of self-discipline and generally speaking, the health risks of such diseases are blatantly obvious yet the sufferer cannot break the cycle. In extreme cases, individuals resort to invasive surgery in an attempt to stop their over-eating. The people who suffer such diseases can be said to be gluttonous, as they have lost control of their eating habits, their lifestyle and their health. In a society where crime rates are relatively low, preventable illnesses subsequent to gluttony, quite dramatically kill more than the sword.

To be gluttonous is to live a life in excess, to be greedy and selfish. Whether the glutton's vice be food, drink or wealth, such overindulgence can be deadly. Ultimately, when self-control is lost to feed one's desires, gluttony is at its most hazardous. Today, gluttony kills more than any other means. In most cases, morbidity is attributable to a deficiency of self-discipline. Both directly and indirectly, gluttony causes more deaths than the sword, the gun, the accident. According to Proverb, 'And put a knife to thy throat, if thou be a man given to appetite.'

THOUGHT AND CONTENT

Strengths

Your effort to establish a link between the gluttony of the ancient world and the contemporary one shows a a talent for creativity that will be an asset in future writing.

Areas for Improvement

The essay is not particularly thought-provoking, nor does it offer much in the way of persuasion. In encapsulating your main idea within this sentence:. *More subtle than the sword, gluttony kills and it does so in greater numbers,* which appears to be your thesis statement, you have fallen into not one, but two pitfalls facing the unwary student who wants to write a stimulating and thought-provoking argumentative essay:

Pitfall No. 1 : Topic is older than Methuselah.

Pitfall No. 2: Not much inherent controversy (if any).

1) Topic: A topic that is very familiar has some huge pitfalls: the fact that it's familiar means it's hard to say anything new: and this particular subject: "too much of a good thing," or perhaps a more up-to-date specific variant such as "Don't eat so much, you'll get fat" or, more direct: "You'll be obese and die young of a heart attack."

-- might even be among the top 10 of well-known phrases people in Western society have heard since childhood.

2) The issue of controversy: You decided to write an argumentative essay: Why? Do you remember how your study guide, "The Guru Method," frames the purpose of that format? Here it is: "The argumentative essay requires you to take a position, explain it (the position) and use reasons to consolidate it." Note that taking a position is equivalent to the phrase "taking sides" -- and so this format works best — no, better said, it only works —when there are actually two sides to an issue.

Suggestions

Questions to ask yourself after selecting a quote and a topic based on it: Are there two sides to it? For example, cast your mind back to the moment you decided to write about gluttony, and narrowed that down to present-day obesity (leaving out the ancient world, which just complicates things.) If you want to write convincingly about the evils of current gluttony (as covered in your 3rd paragraph), do you think there is an opposing argument? Are you going to find many people in your target audience (consisting of academics assigned to evaluate your writing efforts) who would get all fired up and, if they were free to do so, would respond with counter-arguments about how they think it's just a fine idea for people to keep on eating as much as they want — because all that talk about obesity being a problem is just baseless nonsense? They are the people you need to convince.

ORGANISATION AND EXPRESSION

Strengths

The writing style you adopted for this piece is adequate for the purpose.

Areas for Improvement

(1) Overlong paragraphs; this has been discussed in an earlier analysis done for you.

(2) Your 2 introductory sentences, rather than drawing the reader in, are a bit off-putting. You say, *Christianity defines gluttony as one of the seven deadly sins. Therefore, an overconsumption of food, drink or money is obviously dangerous.* Again, consider your target audience when you write. In this instance, you give the impression that you are writing to a specific audience: an audience of Christians.

Saying that Christianity defines a word in such-and-such a way, and concluding that *Therefore* such-and-such must be true, is appropriate for a Christian magazine intended for Christian believers, but….all you can possibly know about the marker for your Gamsat is that the person is well-educated. It might be more prudent to use the common "dictionary" for your source of definition, rather than any of the sacred texts of any particular religion.

Suggestions

Even though your breadth of knowledge about a topic may be considerable, showing off that knowledge by writing down as much background information about the topic as you can think of in as short a time as possible is not what will get you a good mark. Although knowledge about the topic is indeed vital, imparting that knowledge to your reader , as you did in abundance here, isn't what is needed.

Instead, your job is, first, to narrow down your topic to a controversial aspect of that topic. Second, ascertain whether you can not only formulate a thesis, but can identify in your mind the counter-arguments your target audience would have. Third, it's your job to convine your reader, using your vast knowledge of the topic to come up with supporting evidence to substantiate your thesis.

The one single promising way to improve your next essay:

Convincing" is the keyword for an argumentative essay.

ESSAY TWO

To eat is human, to digest divine.

A normal characteristic of human behaviour is to eat. Being able to digest that food is an extra step that implies the enjoyment of what is being eaten beyond the process of mastication. 'To eat is human, to digest divine', I see this as a metaphor which distinguishes ordinary people from those that are extraordinary.

In our society we have our celebrities and our heroes, indeed these people deserve our commendations, however the common person can also have the ability to change and affect peoples' lives. Role models are such people, as well as those individuals who in common society influence change in others.

The personal fitness trainer in particular is an individual who people aspire to become because they display a set of values that people tend to revere in our society. People respect them because they epitomise what is means to be healthy through their fit appearance and role model attitudes for professionalism, compassion and the desire to succeed. These are traits that people idolise and attempt to incorporate into their own lives, somewhat affecting a change in outlook and life implementation along the way.

Having the ability to influence and affect change in others is an extraordinary act that not all can do. To be idolised and remembered to the point that people change their own behaviours is a form of power that the ordinary can't do.

THOUGHT AND CONTENT

Strengths

The line of thought is clearly expressed and therefore easy to follow and understand.

Areas for Improvement

(1) The essay reads like an abstract. (The definition of the word "abstract," when used as a noun, is: "a written summary of an article or a book.")

(2) Just as in your earlier attempts at writing an argumentative essay, you have made assertions in this piece that apparently represent your strongly-held beliefs, seemingly without any concern about whether what you're putting down on paper has the capacity to convince a reader of the validity of the claims you make. To be more specific: You have failed to provide even the most minimal credible, specific evidence of any sort that: *people aspire to be fitness trainers*, that: *people respect them*, that: *people idolise them*, that: *people attempt to incorporate their traits into their own lives, somewhat effecting a change in outlook*.....

Suggestions

Perhaps the explanations and suggestions for improvement in the earlier analyses written for you were not clear, or not detailed enough. So, let's try to be more specific about how you can make sure you have included the really important element of any argumentative essay, which is: the evidence that must be provided for your words to be convincing.

In one of those analyses, you were advised to: "...imagine the other person, shaking his head and asking questions such as "Why do you say that?" "How do you know?" "Who says so, besides you?" "Did you just dream that up?" "Give me one example!" Now, let's apply that advice to the writing of the present essay. When you wrote: *People respect them because they epitomise what is means to be healthy through their fit appearance and role model attitudes for professionalism*..... you were making an assertion. But how could you make that claim so confidently? What's clear is only that *you* respect fitness trainers, but for all we readers know, you may be the only person in the world who does.

Now, you might be asking at this point, "How could I have been more specific?" Here's just *one* way: you could have mentioned statements you have read or heard made by certain people who have enthusiastically praised their trainers. For example, perhaps you could quote a noted sports celebrity who has publicly mentioned something like this: "I'd be nothing it if weren't for my trainer...he's my idol."

And if your next question is, "But what if I can't think of any factual evidence?" then the answer to that is...Choose a different topic to write an argumentative essay about; you're not going to be able to write a convincing argumentative essay on this topic.

ORGANISATION AND EXPRESSION

Strengths

Your writing shows a level of skill that is more than adequate for the task you undertook.

Areas for Improvement

(1) Your structural framework is very weak; the essay, organisationally speaking, is out of balance. You've presented a very, very brief piece of writing, which is not necessarily a flaw in itself, but in this case, you've taken 2 full paragraphs (out of only 4 paragraphs in the

entire piece) to plod through an introduction. You only get to the meat of your argument in the 3rd paragraph, and that's it! The entire thesis and supporting evidence—the end-all and be-all—which ordinarily take up the first 4 paragraphs of a 5-paragraph essay, are smashed and jammed into one single paragraph here.

You took 2 paragraphs out of the 4 to get to the point because you chose to base your argument for this essay on a very convoluted interpretation of the quote you chose. So, although the explanation you provided in those first two paragraphs was clear, taking up that much space and time does not seem to have been a wise decision to have made in the planning stage, in view of the fact that it was going to take up almost half your essay.

(2) The above deals with "organisation;" however, your "expression" could bear some improvement as well. Your initial sentence in any piece of writing should be carefully crafted with an eye to "hooking" the reader, which means saying something that will entice the reader or arouse his or her curiosity —something calculated to draw the reader on to read more. Now, here's the first sentence of your present essay: *A normal characteristic of human behaviour is to eat.* Given your evident abilities, don't you think you could have come up with something a bit more appealing?

Suggestions

In addition to the suggestion above (in the "Thought and Content" section) that you might use comments made by certain individuals as one of the ways to provide supportive evidence for your claims, there's another very simple-to-remember reason to include anecdotes about individuals, or just their comments. Whenever you come across a piece of writing that has as its central theme some aspect of human behaviour, but only speaks about it in generalities, such as "people tend to do this or that," and never refers to even one real person as an example to make its point —you're looking at a piece of writing that's guaranteed to bore you.

The one single promising way to improve your next essay:

Planning is the key. Take planning seriously, and know the content of each sentence within each paragraph before you put pen to paper.

ESSAY THREE

There is nothing to which men, while they have food and drink, cannot reconcile themselves.

George Santayana

(Just a question - what does 'eating is touch carried to the bitter end' mean?)

Food nourishes the soul as it does the body. By satisfying our physical needs our minds are made ready to reconcile tensions with other people or the situations in which we find ourselves. This emotional process is made possible by the chemistry of the brain. Through the positive physical and emotional powers of food, man is able to find peace and reconciliation in whatever area of life so requests it.

Food is strongly associated with memories of lesuirely times spent in communal harmony. I find that the taste of jam sandwiches instantly invokes a heady nostalgic feeling. It reminds me of picnics with my family and lunchbox days with school friends. For many people, food conjures memories of peaceful times, easing them into a state conducive to reconciliation with others.

The emotions which are aroused by food stem from the biochemical and biological effects of food. Well-known are the effects of tryptophan and serotonin, chemicals found in certain foods which are implicated in a sense of calmness and peace. A sense of serenity is crucial to the reconciliation of oneself to an otherwise upsetting situation. The process of reconciliation necessarily bypasses the frontal lobe of the brain, comprised on neurons running on the sustenance which the body receives through food. When it is provided with food and drink, it is able to achieve reconciliation.

I have personally dealt with an eating disorder in the past. In that time, I manipulated my intake of food to reconcile myself to the parts of me I could not accept and the environment I could not control. During my recovery, I realised that food was the key to reconciling myself to my own physical body and to my insecurities. To myself and many others, food has been the iron which has helped to straighten out the imperfections of this world.

Food is essential to the functioning of humans. It is not the be-all-and-end-all solution in the face of the fractured relationships of man. However, the positive associations and the neural effects of the nutrition provided by food fortify its role in the reconciliation of man to that which troubles the soul.

THOUGHT AND CONTENT

Strengths

You present a clear, concise thesis statement in the final sentence of the first paragraph.

Areas for Improvement

The relatively static level of "quality of thought" of the entire essay is the underlying weakness of this piece of writing. The basic concept of the essay is simple, and while simplicity is desirable in an essay, it alone is not enough to make an essay rise above average. And in this case, the problem is over-simplification, aggravated by repetitiveness. Not until the conclusion do you falter in your absolutism, your "one-note" praise of food as a sort of panacea for the troubled soul, and even then, you do so only in passing as you recognize, a bit late in the game, that food *is not the be-all-and-end-all solution.*

Here are a few of the reasons why your claim that *Through the positive physical and emotional powers of food, man is able to find peace and reconciliation in whatever area of life so requests it* is not persuasive:

1) Your claim to the universality of the power of food is in no way proven. While you quote scientific knowledge about the calming effects of certain chemicals in some foods, there is no evidence provided that this is universally true, or if it's even effective when a person is suffering not just malaise, but a genuine crisis, whether mental or physical, momentary or prolonged.

2) Attention to the concept of eating as a palliative for one's distress is front and center these days, but not in the glowing terms you view it; rather, what is being spotlighted is the

a concern that the growing problem of obesity is, at least in some people, the result of the very thing you are talking about — eating "comfort food" instead of tackling the person's real underlying problems in such a way as to help solve them.

3) Your claim of universality is also counterintuitive, in that there are many people who cannot eat at all when going through a crisis…..as we often see in cases where, when the situation is immediate, some people, if pressed to eat, cannot keep any food down. And there are also many who, if experiencing a prolonged period of anxiety, tend to drop weight precipitously even though plenty of food is available—apparently because they do not experience the effect you describe as finding *peace and reconciliation in whatever area of life so requests it.*

Suggestions

While providing scientific evidence in an effort to substantiate your major claims can often be very effective in an argumentative essay, you must be very careful when doing so. Physical scientists are generally very conscientious when reporting the results of their studies; they try to avoid drawing any conclusions that can be interpreted as sweeping generalizations. That being the case, whoever the scientists were who provided information on the effect of food on the chemistry of the brain, it's quite possible they might recoil from your first paragraph, in which you seemingly empower food to be the end-all-and be-all (a sweeping generalization that is not denied until the conclusion).

ORGANISATION AND EXPRESSION

Strengths

Forgetting for a moment the complaint, above, regarding the lack of persuasiveness, your writing is quite expressive and manages to convey the strength of your own convictions.

Areas for Improvement

1) Although there are improvements in clarity over your earlier essays, you have not yet managed to completely eliminate convoluted sentences that are, unfortunately, incomprehensible, as in: *The process of reconciliation necessarily bypasses the frontal lobe of the brain, comprised on neurons running on the sustenance which the body receives through food.*

2) Your example about your eating disorder failed to contribute in any significant way to your thesis because it was written in a way as if you intended to appear clouded in mystery.

And that's a pity, because the idea of using your own experience could have really enhanced the total picture; after all, you were following the advice given in your study guide, The Guru, which says: "The most powerful reflections are personal ones; it would be very helpful if you could write about personal experiences that serve to illustrate themes in the quote. Even if the reflections are not personal ones, write about them as if they were."

While the idea behind providing your own experience is that this is a way of connecting with the reader on a human basis, much like a personal letter to a friend. And while you achieved this kind of connection with an entire paragraph by means of the simple reference to the taste of jam sandwiches, your paragraph on the eating disorder—which obviously would have been more important because it delved to a deeper level—you failed with the eating disorder. The latter, as mentioned above, seems to be purposely vague, as if you

were a prevaricating teenager being confronted by a parent, and you were loath to provide much information for fear of being punished.

Suggestions

(1) Many of the criticisms above, both in the "Thought and Content" portion of the analysis and in this section as well, could have been averted if you had realized, after having chosen your topic, that you had all the makings of a reflective essay, which could have been built based on your experience with your eating disorder, The two great advantages in this particular case is that the reflective format ideals in emotion primarily and therefore does not require credible evidence, nor does it abhor sweeping generalizations if they are meant merely to describe your own feelings.

(2) Avoid getting caught in a trap of your own making, as you seem to have done here, allowing yourself to be so bewitched by the phrasing in the quote you chose, that you ended up letting it dominate your entire essay. Specifically, the problem is with the word "reconcile."

While you don't need to know anything about the authors of the quotes that are provided as stimuli on the list of quotes you select from, clues to the era the author of the quote can sometimes be found in the language used. Santayana, in the quote you chose, used the expression "There is nothing to which...men cannot reconcile themselves." So, even if you know nothing about Santayana, you might have been able to discern that he was not a man of our era. In other words, would you expect any article in a contemporary piece of everyday, non-academic writing to use such formal-sounding language?

Presumably not...which is why it is not clear why you used this same language repeatedly, to the point of its being overwhelming— with either "reconcile" or "reconciliation" appearing 9 times in the essay, not counting the original quote(!)

So, here is how you can avoid that trap: Don't get over-involved with the quote. The quotations are only there as a stimulus to thought; you don't have to view it as a statement that you either have to agree with or disagree with, and you don't have to adhere to its phrasing.

The one single promising way to improve your next essay:

Keep your target audience in mind: for these essays, both the practice ones and the Gamsat, that audience is a marker who, first of all, wants to be able to read your piece through smoothly without having to stop because of incomprehensible sentences, and second, is looking for something interesting and credible -- possibly also refreshing, something that makes him/her go on thinking over what you've said for some time after reading it. Or perhaps, after reading it, saying simply, "I never thought of it that way,"

ESSAY FOUR

"You may as well be spooning out cyanide!" I protested profusely and consistently for months on end. Flax seed oil, like the rest of the uber health food store ingredients we'd recently been stocking, seemed to be less of a fad than I had hoped for.

In the early days of this new diet craze, I was still identifying with poor Mr Asimov, finding to my dismay that every time I was enjoying that angelic burger of mouth watering dessert, I was "torturing my body". Oh the frustration! Torture? If this were torture, I have no idea why the UN is doubtful of the US's 'enhanced interrogation techniques'. Enjoyment of food is enjoyment of life, that is a promise. By how this enjoyment can manifest in different dressings was the holy grail to my yet uneaten courses.

My Dad diagnosed with prostate cancer. The stressful operation and worrisome recovery. The joyful news of a positive result. The irksome food regime? Quite the unexpected, out of left field twist to the story. We all took on Dad's new eating habits. As stated earlier, not too keenly. Over time I noted my progression towards enjoying wholesome foods, and turning my nose up at junk foods. Assuredly I still feel the pull towards a greasy treat, but the post hunger dissonance is clearly one of disgust – I not only feel guilty, but queezy from the splurge. A by product of my Dad's new diet is my own nullification of deriving enjoyment from bad foods. The key result: my Dad's exceedingly strong immune system; my palate linking good with healthy.

Wait there's more to this! Food's food, we all need this. I propose that moderation in all forms of life is key to enjoyment. There's 'too much of a good thing', and also 'devilishly bad'. We can decide watching movie's would be quite a satisfactory way to spend the rest of our working days. We could choose the over budget house with amazing views. We could opt for all sexual fantasies to be granted, perhaps by access to a genie in a bottle. Those ingratiated with such luck of these sorts, eventually grow tired of their movies/views/hedonistic pleasures.

Like the bad food which still has flavours that are tasty, the enjoyment only lasts while the experience is fleeting. Moderation in all aspects of life allows us to be happy with our equilibrium state – occasionally we can lash out and watch movies when they're not supposed to, or take in those spectacular views, but saturation leads to boredom, much unlike saturated fats leading to longevity.

THOUGHT AND CONTENT

Strengths

The points made in the final two paragraphs were a good start in the right direction.

Areas for Improvement

If the reader is patient and is willing to stick with your piece faithfully to the end, then his or her faithfulness will be rewarded by what finally comes through as, apparently, the lesson you would like the reader to believe you learned from your entire dietary modification process. That point appears to be: *Moderation in all forms of life is key to enjoyment.*

However, nothing in your entire essay up to that point (at almost the end of the piece) seems relevant to that lesson. Rather, you report not that you have learned to eat all types of food, including unhealthy foods, <u>in moderation</u>, but rather that you learned to abstain from unhealthy foods because of a feeling of guilt-plus-=queasiness after eating them. So you've gone for total abstinence, evidently. No moderation there.

Suggestions

Unless you can manage to control your creative writing urge, it might be better in the long run for you to forsake it (the humor, that is) altogether — and concentrate instead on producing an essay in which your creativity is channeled into a piece of writing that features serious quality of thought exclusively.

Writing in a light, humorous vein, as you did, is a great idea, if you can carry it off well and still get your serious point across. However, as you may know, most comedy writers and actors, when interviewed about their craft, indicate that comedy is far more difficult to do successfully than drama or anything else that is just plain serious.

ORGANISATION AND EXPRESSION

Strengths

Considered as a whole, the essay is quite engaging.

Areas for Improvement

Lack of clarity in some parts of the essay causes confusion, and because those parts are details that are not particularly vital, the lack of clarity ultimately, leads the reader to want to skim through the piece, looking for major points that are clear. This, of course, is not a desirable outcome from your point of view, because in skipping some parts, the reader may miss the most important idea that you wanted to get across.

One example of this lack of clarity is the fact that you devote two entire paragraphs to a fanciful description of your reaction to a *new diet craze,* and then the next paragraph switches abruptly to the serious subject of your father's diagnosis, and your statement that *We all took on Dad's new eating habits.* The confusion here is that the reader doesn't know whether the *new diet craze* and *Dad's new eating habits* happen concurrently, or are simply one and the same.

You say, *Quite the unexpected, out of left field twist to the story,* which contributes to making the sequence of events unclear. The initial two paragraphs, referring to a *craze,* and written in a comic style, bring to mind the concept of a "health food nut" running the kitchen and shopping, rather than a person helping a family member follow doctor's orders.

Those two initial paragraphs simply do not comport well with the notion of a serious effort at diet modification that undoubtedly was recommended by medical professionals. In a nutshell: we don't know whether the dietary modifications were already in progress when Dad was diagnosed, or whether the entire changeover took place afterward.

Suggestions

The suggestion here is one that reinforces the suggestion provided above in the "Thought and Content" section of this analysis: that it may be best for you to abandon the effort at humor, because that effort leads you astray. In the matter of the sequence of events out-lined above, you seem to have fallen into the pitfall of enjoying your creative impulse at the expense of clarity of thought.

 For an essay to stand out, apart from the uppermost importance of a well-developed line of thought, it must flow smoothly. Consider an additional example of the problem of sim-ple flaws that, combined, affect your ability to get through to your reader: the transition from the second paragraph to the third paragraph. That transition embodies a complete interruption in the thought process, and is therefore the exact opposite of what is known as a "smooth transition."

The one single promising way to improve your next essay:

Because the evaluation of your essay will be weighted 75% on quality of thought, just re-member it's ultimately easier to achieve quality of thought with a serious approach.

ESSAY TOPICS: TOPIC FOUR

TOPIC FOUR

Consider the following comments and develop a piece of writing in response to one or more of them.

Your writing will be judged on the quality of your response to the theme; how well you organise and present your point of view, and how effectively you express yourself.

You will not be judged on the views or attitudes you express.

****

Most plans are just inaccurate predictions.

Ben Bayol

It is a mistake to look too far ahead. Only one link in the chain of destiny can be handled at a time.

Sir Winston Churchill

Long-range planning works best in the short term

Doug Evelyn

If you plan to win as I do, the game never ends.

Stan Mikita

We always plan too much and always think too little.

Joseph Schumpeter

ESSAYS AND ANALYSES: TOPIC FOUR

ESSAY ONE

"We always plan too much and think too little." – A reflection on mortality and parenthood.

Others had warned me it might feel like this.

Staring into the inky pools of my newborn son's eyes for the first time, I felt as though the earth had stopped turning. The hum of the hospital faded to a murmur, the fog of labour lifted and there was only he and I in the room.

It was, I imagined later, not un-similar to the experience of death. The moment when everything stops, not only for the dying but for those left behind and mourning the end of the relationship, as W.H Auden wrote, "let the clocks stop turning."

My life before I had children was very much a future-focused affair. The next holiday, the next job, party to attend, book to read, meal to eat. Sure, I thought about important things, social justice issues and the state of the planet but rarely did I dwell on my own mortality.

Now I think about it, and what it means, almost every day.

"Life is what happens when you are busy making other plans," John Lennon sang to his own newborn son. Making plans is one way of avoiding thinking about life and death. However, it is only through thinking about life, and death on a regular basis that we can really value the gift of existence and make plans to honour it.

Those who live by a Buddhist philosophy have long been puzzled by the western preoccupation with time and planning. For them, age is non-consequential, you are born and then you die and there is no need to mark the points in between.

Young children, by their nature are similar. They live very much in the present moment, the meal they are eating right now, the game they are playing. Putting their shoes on to go outside is a major exercise in planning and logistics.

Joseph Schumpeter was neither a child nor a Buddhist but his reflection that "plan too much and think too little", takes the best of both ways of living and applies them to modern life.

or without time spent thinking, about consequences beyond the here and now, the plans we make are of little value.

THOUGHT AND CONTENT

Strengths

There is a strong, engaging introduction that motivates the reader to go on, in the hope of learning more.

Areas for Improvement

There's an engrossing buildup and then, overall, a big letdown after the first 3 short paragraphs. A great beginning for a reflective essay; However, once you've hooked the reader, you fail to deliver what should have been the meat of the piece.

Perhaps a comparative example will help you understand: Imagine that someone you see on a daily basis— a family member, a roommate, a co-worker,— says to you, out of the blue: "We ought to give some thought to the way we interact, you know, the way we relate to each other." How would you react? If you were to say, "OK, good idea," wouldn't you expect the person to fill you in on the details? What exactly does he or she have in mind, what kinds of issues, etc.? But in this example, the person says, when prompted, "Oh, I meant it's very important to just think about how we interact."

Your essay tells the reader the same– just substitute "mortality" for "how we interact."

This is quite disappointing. After drawing the reader in, you abandon the personal touch so necessary for a successful reflective essay, and go off into philosophizing, speaking exclusively in generalities about life and death. And then, what's even more vexing to the reader, you go off the personal track completely, talking about Buddhists' and children's understanding of the world. Not a word about your own. Where, in all this, is to be found the meat of a reflective essay?

Suggestions

To quote from The Guru Method: "A reflective essay is quite personal….." Your personal approach stopped abruptly after the sentence *Now I think about it, and what it means, almost every day*….at the exact point where the reader expects you to fill in the details, and reveal the how and why you came to your current belief. All you have essentially shared with the reader is your statement that before you had the baby, *rarely did I dwell on my own mortality* and your current belief that *without time spent thinking, about consequences beyond the here and now, the plans we make are of little value.* How you got from one belief to the other remains a grand mystery and represents a huge flaw in the essay.

Perhaps once you started in on the essay, you realized that you did not want to share your intimate thoughts. That's quite understandable, but you must consider the element of privacy before you take on the project of a reflective essay

ORGANISATION AND EXPRESSION

Strengths

Your writing certainly expresses the strength of your convictions.

Areas for Improvement

(1) Inasmuch as you are, to the best of the reader's knowledge, not a prophet nor a revered seer, you aren't going to impress your target audience for these essays with

a statement such as you wrote in your conclusion: *For without time spent thinking, about consequences beyond the here and now, the plans we make are of little value.* It just sounds pompous — unless you back it up with something that tells us why you believe this is so, and by extension, why you're trying to convince the reader that it is so.

(2) Another way in which the essay is deficient in the area of organisation: All of the essays you have submitted to date appear rather fdaunting at first glance, because you do not bother to put a decent space between your paragraphs. Actually, it's not a small thing, because first impressions are sometimes crucial, and the first impression one gets from just looking at your essay is that it's a solid mass of print and is going to be a chore to read.

Suggestions

Re: it is only through thinking about life, and death on a regular basis that we can really value the gift of existence and make plans to honour it.

Beware of writing sentences that begin: "It is only through_____that we can… ….."

This kind of warning, intended as a bit of wisdom that the author, apparently innocently and earnestly, intends to impart, can be very annoying. It is dogmatic, telling the reader there is <u>only one way</u>, and guess what? That way, wouldn't you know, just happens to be the way the author chooses to believe.

A religious person may write: "It is only through prayer and devotion that we can ever attain our desires." That could be quite annoying to an atheist; however, the non-believing reader would have nothing to complain about if the writer had simply used a different set of pronouns: "I" and "my" instead of "we" and "our." For example: "I've found that the only way I can achieve my goals in life is through prayer and devotion…"

The one single promising way to improve your next essay:

Whether you choose the argumentative or the reflective format, you must avoid trying to make points by sweeping generalities, but rather, you must provide supportive material that explains in detail the point you are trying to make.

....

ESSAY TWO

'Long-range planning works best in the short term.'

Doug Evelyn

Long range planning rarely goes according to plan and is always pinned to predictions regarding future circumstances. It often achieves many short-term benefits, but its real efficacy hinges on unpredictable factors which may or may not confer success.

If we take a look at Australia's history, we will come to a time when there were fears of rising levels of immigration. The politicians of the time decided to tackle this matter head on and nip the issue in the bud to prevent serious damage from occurring in the long term. The result was the Immigration Restriction Act, which aimed to prevent the migration of undesirable people. What the politicians of the time did not raise was that the world would rapidly shift in values, with global borders lifting. A multicultural Australia would have been beneficial to the national economy. While the restriction of 'undesirable' ethnicities placed Anglo-Saxon Australians at ease in the short term, they suffered for it in later years. Yet there was little chance that at the time, they would correctly predict the way in which the world would change. It is only logical to base plans for the future on what we see in the present, but unfortunately, circumstances change without warning.

Long range planning sometimes fails to account for the intricacies which surround the plan. Particularly in times of desperation we are susceptible to the trap of heading for the solution which looks as if it will alleviate the problem. When cane beetles plagued plagued Queensland backyards, environmentalists declared that the solution was the cane toad. It was considered the long-term solution for pest control. It was not considered that these toads could be damaging to native species and domestic pets. Long range planning sometimes works best to ease peoples' anxieties in the present. It fails to take into account the problems of a few years.

In the light of these examples, we recognise that the Australian government's proposition to raise the retirement age to 70 may sound appropriate, given the present situation. The perceived inability to take care of pensioners would support a greater retirement age, but there is no guarantee that the demographics will reflect today's. Addtionally, there have been a general reaction against the notion of retiring at the age of seventy. This is a case in which planning may not be good in the long term, or even in the short term.

Successful long range planning, even when executed with skill and insight, cannot fully claim guaranteed success in the future. Decisions based on present conditions have the ability to solve today's problems but the dynamics of the world in which we live in are known to no one. The enigma of the future is the insurmountable hurdle posed to long range planning.

THOUGHT AND CONTENT

Strengths

The line of thought is well-developed and the essay flows smoothly—showing, overall, marked improvement over your previous submissions.

Areas for Improvement

The persuasive power is lukewarm because your argument is flawed. The entire piece could've been stronger if you'd taken the trouble to refine your argument and come up with a strong position. Unfortunately, however, in setting forth a thesis statement that says: *its real efficacy hinges on unpredictable factors which may or may not confer success,* the only position you've actually taken is a position of neutrality. You're neither for nor against the usefulness of long-range planning. Not to mention the fact that this statement is very far from having the compelling "punch" you need to draw in your reader.

With that thesis statement presented in the first paragraph, and repeated in your conclusion, you are announcing that what you are going to persuade your reader of is that no one can ever fully guarantee the success of any plan because of the unpredictability factor. But why did you think we, your reader(s), needed to be convinced of that? Didn't we know that already?

To help you understand this criticism, please consider the requirements of the argumentative essay, as succinctly laid out in your study guide, The Guru Method: "An argumentative essay requires you to....take a position, explain it (the position), and use reasons to consolidate it." Clearly, the implication of "taking a position" is that the issue to be discussed is somewhat controversial — controversial enough that there are at least two easily identifiable sides.

Now, to be specific, taking a closer look at the position you've taken, can you see why the question asked above about why your reader needs to be convinced comes up: who, in your target audience for this particular essay —an audience presumably consisting of adults—would argue with such a position? Who would say, "No, I don't agree! I think it's quite possible that any long-range planning, if done expertly, will always work perfectly and without a hitch." You see, you've structured your essay in such a way that you've ended up "taking sides" when there is actually only one side.

Suggestions

The above does not mean that there was no other way to go, given the topic you chose. On the contrary: the issue of the value of long-term planning is rich with possibilities for genuine controversial argument. In the planning stage, if you'd taken more time to examine the issue and fine-tune your position, you might have come up with a much stronger argument. See below, under the "Suggestions" heading of the "Organisation and Expression" section.

ORGANISATION AND EXPRESSION

Strengths

The greatest strength in the "Organisation" of the essay is the third example you provided, which built on the two previous examples. Having dealt with long-term planning episodes that occurred in the past in those two paragraphs, you made an interesting, insightful transition to the present with the third example. You enhanced the feel and tone by bringing a living, breathing issue into the discussion.

Areas for Improvement

The first sentence of the essay is misleading and unsupported by fact, and both of these things are caused by lack of attention to detail. The sentence is misleading because your theme is not the frequency of failure of long-term planning (in fact, you never mention frequency again except vaguely, as in *sometime)s*. It's also unsupported because you provide no statistics about how often this type of planning fails. The first sentence of any essay should be carefully worded in order to give the reader a hint about what's to come.

Suggestions

Regarding ways to come up with a stronger argument, as mentioned above: You could have decided that— since you're not writing for a middle school audience, but rather for a target audience that already knows the basics concerning the impossibility of perfect outcomes of long-term planning—you'd have to toss your original idea for a thesis statement. But you can use that knowledge your reader obviously has as a basis, and build on it to formulate an issue which does have two sides.

How about this, for instance: since one can assume agreement on the fact that perfect outcomes can't be predicted, one position might be: "I'm opposed to our government engaging in long-term planning because the fact that you can't know the future renders such planning useless and therefore a waste of time and money."

Or, you could choose the other side: "I'm strongly in favor of long-term planning because you can't run a government properly if you fail to consider future needs, and the fact that we can't predict with accuracy simply means that not only do we have to plan carefully, but that is only the beginning, because we also must have Plan B, and Plan C worked out as well."

The one single promising way to improve your next essay:

Take time to formulate your thesis statement carefully, and then make sure it is foolproof.

ESSAY TOPICS: TOPIC FIVE

TOPIC FIVE

Consider the following comments and develop a piece of writing in response to one or more of them.

Your writing will be judged on the quality of your response to the theme; how well you organise and present your point of view, and how effectively you express yourself.

You will not be judged on the views or attitudes you express.

* * * * * * *

Honor is the reward of virtue.

Marcus Tullius Cicero

The louder he talked of his honor, the faster we counted our spoons.

Ralph Waldo Emerson

Without money honor is merely a disease.

Jean Racine

Honor has not to be won; it must only not be lost.

Arthur Schopenhauer

It is better to die on your feet than to live on your knees!

Emiliano Zapata

ESSAYS AND ANALYSES: TOPIC FIVE

....

ESSAY ONE

Honour is the reward of virtue.

Honour and virtue are words that often come hand in hand. The definitions of each of the words virtue and honour are what allow these words to be coupled in the way that they are. By definition honour many be said to be a state of honesty and virtue may be said to be carrying out actions of high moral standing. From these definitions we can conclude that honour is directly linked to virtue but how do the human race define these moral codes? What do we define to be an act of goodness?

While it is most definitely correct to say that honour is the reward of virtue we must also examine what exactly virtue is defined as. There is no definition of what the codes of virtue are. They have been defined by the human race and often there are huge variations in what would be considered as honourable acts, from region to region or continent to continent. Is an act of virtue today seen as the ability to fight for your country in which case for those that cannot face standing in war for their country, they may be considered to be disloyal and in effect selfish people. This draws me to the concept of military conscription. In continents such as South America as well Russia military conscription exists today, while in developed regions such as North America conscription is enforced when necessary. This is one of the things which the human race today would perceive as an act of high moral standing, an act of virtue. It is indeed an act of honour but the case could be examined in a different way. Where people are serving overseas to fight for their country, they are engaging in war, all being for the sake if their country. In fighting for the country lives are being lost and war very often sees no end. When examined in this way, how can serving time in a war be seen as an act of goodness.

Honour is a word that is mentioned often in a praising light of someone. Acts of honour can too vary from region to region. An example of this may be seen in the different religions. For example in the Muslim religion there is no limit to the number of wives a man can have whereas in Catholicism, having any more than one wife at any one time is seen as a sin and would be very frowned upon in society.

Certain aspects of the way people live their lives, are globally and culturally accepted as doing good. Veronica Guerins death for example in 1996 highlighted the most honourable character that she was, owing her life to combating drugs in

Ireland. The same applies to Diana, princess of Wales, who spent much of her life in underdeveloped regions caring for malnourished sick people and often young children. In light of the above it is very clear that honour is indeed a reward of virtue however cultural differences can often impede on what exactly virtue is defined as. An act of goodness, as carried out by people like Diana and Veronica Guerin, will without fail have influence on the honour associated with a person. These actions such as helping those in need are recognised as acts of virtue whether it be in Ireland or in Africa, regardless of race, religion or cultural differences.

Contradictory to the above, one may argue that honour is not always the reward of virtue. This is a very true statement. Virtue is hugely associated with honesty. Very often highly commended people should never have been rewarded the honour that they are given. Lance Armstrong for example recently admitted that his success throughout his career was due to the concoction of performance enhancing drugs which he took. Throughout Armstrong's life he was seen as a man of great honour. Where was the virtue in what Armstrong did? His life was a sin. He earned enormous amounts of money and gained a huge amount of public respect during his time performing. Unfortunately this is not the only case where honour has wrongly been rewarded to a person.

It may be seen from the above that honour is the reward of virtue whether virtue is seen as serving overseas in a war to fight on behalf of a country or whether virtue is seen as the ability to cycle and win hundreds of races worldwide. When referring to each of these examples, there are without doubt two sides of the argument however in all cases the person is seen as a person of huge honour. While the lies and sin that Armstrong committed today shock his loving followers, for the time that he won all races he was seen as a man of great honour. A soldier in fighting for his country is seen as a man of great honour and not one that is taking the lives of others. The ability to earn honour is defined by what we perceive as virtue. Virtue is indeed an act of doing good but it can often be the case that what one may see as being an act off goodness, another may see as being an act of none other than evil. Despite this, where virtue as the public perceive it, is in instilled within a person, honour will inevitably be rewarded.

THOUGHT AND CONTENT

Strengths

This is an earnest attempt to interpret a rather inscrutable quote in terms of contemporary society's values.

Areas for Improvement

(1) The essay wanders. By "wandering," what is meant is that, just as you did in a previous effort, you opened up with a couple of questions, such as a teacher does when trying to stimulate a class of students to think. Again, as in your earlier piece, there is no thesis statement at the outset.

Instead of letting the reader know in your introductory paragraph what your exact topic is going to be and how you are going to attack it, it is not until the conclusion that you give any hint of a summation of any kind. That hint comes with this sentence: *Virtue is indeed an act of doing good but it can often be the case that what one may see as being an act off goodness, another may see as being an act of none other than evil.*

(2) As indicated to you in an earlier analysis, the recommended vehicle for effectively displaying your power of intellect is the essay. You again apparently intended to write an argumentative essay. In that format, the writer emphatically takes one side of an issue, as opposed to what you've done here, which seems to be an effort to be objective and discuss the pros and cons of each side. This piece of writing, therefore, reads very much like a letter one might write to a friend, turning over some ideas in the writer's mind. You go back and forth, exploring the issue, which gives the impression that this might be the first time you've ever thought about the whole complexity of the issue, and certainly not like a presentation of a well-thought-out argument.

Suggestions

(1) All of the critical comment in the above comments should not be interpreted as simply being a matter of the format. That is, it might seem to you that you're being criticized because you didn't write the first paragraph in such-and-such a way, etc. What the comments above are trying to tell you is that your wandering results in a considerable lack of clarity. If you want someone to become interested in what you have to say, the first requirement is that you have to say it clearly.

(2) While providing definitions in an introductory paragraph is quite acceptable, any definition you give ought to be carefully crafted so that it clearly applies to what you intend to say in the remainder of the essay. Your definition of "honour" as *a state of honesty* is quite misleading, because in the material that follows, your usage of the word is in the sense of "respect" being afforded to a person, and not to one's honesty.

ORGANISATION AND EXPRESSION

Strengths

Your mechanics (grammar, sentence structure) are adequate to express your views.

Areas for Improvement

A lack of adequate planning is quite likely the root cause of the wandering. You may be feeling a bit indignant, as you read this, because you feel that you did indeed work out a plan. If that is true, then perhaps the question is, was the planning adequate?

You should understand that it is not only the above-mentioned factors — lack of thesis statement, wandering, lack of clarity — that are evidence of a lack of planning. Further evidence is provided by the extreme length of this submission. It would take a very polished and experienced writer to come up with an essay of that length that is at the same time also cogent, coherent, and worthy of a high mark — all within a time frame of 30 minutes flat.

Suggestions

(1) Consider the advice given on Page 10 of *The Guru Method*: "The first five minutes should be used to plan, the next twenty to write and the final five minutes to revise any error in thinking or mechanics." As you can see, if you were to follow this advice, you would have to limit yourself to only 20 minutes to do the actual writing.

Now, consider the following comparison: The word count of your piece, according to the standard computer word-counting tool, is a full 200 words longer than the high-mark model

essays provided in *The Guru Method*. Can you see how your apparent desire to put every single thing you think of into your piece of writing actually defeats your purpose?

An important part of the Planning process is weeding out those items that pop into your head sounding like great ideas, but when considered in the light of whether they contribute

directly to your thesis, do not deserve to be included.

The one single promising way to improve your next essay:

Rewrite this piece completely. That is, attempt to write an entirely new essay using nothing from the piece you submitted other than the same quote. Find a quiet time, set a timer to 30 minutes, and with only the words of the quote and writing materials in front of you, see if you can come up with a more engaging piece, one that flows so smoothly that the reader can read through the entire thing at one go. (The result should be much shorter than this submission, but the hope is that it will also be much better.) You do not necessarily have to submit the result for analysis if you are not pleased with it, but the exercise itself should be worthwhile.

ESSAY TWO

Honor has not to be won; it must only not be lost.

Arthur Schopenhauer

Honor is not like a prize you win or a title you receive. It is something conferred upon you by the people around you. It is the reward for the good qualities you cultivated and above all, maintained for a long time. It is not hard to achieve it and not many people endeavour to reach that level. These facts make the state of 'honor'- the state of being respected - so special.

The most common example is about how we honor our politicians and our leaders. We honor them by recognising their efforts and electing them to lead our community. Honor, in this case, is infectious. It is like a good vibe. If these leaders respect the aspirations and expectations of the people of their community, they shall spread this positive vibe thus upholding the honor conferred upon them. The more these leaders work for the community, the better they spread the magical touch of their reward. They inspire another generation of honourable young leaders. It is like a state that is hard to achieve but should never be lost. If our politicians or leaders spent their valuable time doing dishonourable acts like engaging in corruption, encouraging crime, bribery and red tape, they are losing their honor. More effort and strength of mind is required to maintain the honour than losing it.

Upholding 'the state of honour' requires a strong mind and an iron will power. Honour is the reward of such virtues. The most notable example of how hard it is to uphold the state of honour is of the saints in Christianity. Christians honor them. Many of them were honoured during their lifetime. They were able to live an honourable life in a world full of temptations. They clearly convey the message that it is very hard to persevere in the state of honour.

The very fact that it is hard to retain the state of honour makes this virtue more special. The harder it is to achieve a goal, the sweeter the prize feels like. They say "give respect and take respect". So for us to honour someone we need to have had that feeling within us first, that we were touched and honoured by their humility and compassion. It is like a positive vibe which is passed on from one human being to another. This good feeling will be lost if the people who are the 'role models' lose their honour. Not many people are honoured but the ones who are honoured, are worth it.

THOUGHT AND CONTENT

Strengths

The consistency and lucidity of your line of thought in this essay represent improvement over your previous efforts.

Areas for Improvement

While you have achieved the goal of making a clear thesis statement and following it up with two relevant examples—political leaders and saints— the content of those example paragraphs lacks the specificity that would both give depth to, and add persuasive power to, your argument.

Thus, although you have tried to adhere to previous advice to back up your thesis with supportive examples, you have ended up again relying only on opinion in both of the example paragraphs. Every single sentence that follows your introductory remark that *The most common example is about how we honor our politicians and our leaders* is an assertion. Creative though these ideas may be, they are unsupported.

Suggestions

You created an unusual opportunity for yourself and then, apparently unwittingly, passed it up. To be more specific: first, consider that by the very act of choosing to write about honor as a topic, you've entered the realm of the abstract. On top of that,

as if writing about abstract notions weren't difficult enough, the abstract notion of honor is inseparable from the real world—specifically, humans. In other words, honor is something that is relevant only to humans. And the fact is that very often, it's hard to translate abstract concepts into real-life examples.

But in this case, since you created a somewhat novel way of looking at honor as something "conferred" by someone else—rather than, say, a way of looking at it as a concept internally created by the individual about himself based on his own values—you actually made it easy to bridge the gap between an abstract notion and a person. You established a point of view that says honor is something that can be viewed from the outside, so to speak, thus making it possible to give real-life examples of people upon whom honor had been conferred by others, as well as real-life examples of people who had lost it.

That is the opportunity that you missed this time, but should not pass up in the future.

(See more detail about this under "Organisation and Expression" below.)

ORGANISATION AND EXPRESSION

Strengths

Overall, the structural framework, which features fluid transitions, contributes to the smooth flow of the essay, and facilitates a quick read-through.

Areas for Improvement

Although your quality of thought is remarked upon above, you are still in need of improvement in order to raise your mark to above average.

(1) Unnecessary repetitiveness to the point that it is irritating: the third paragraph is so repetitive—repeating the same introductory remarks in different ways—that it ends up containing only a few substantive sentences intended to serve as the example. Actually, the repetitive sentences begin with the last sentence of the 1st paragraph: *More effort and strength of mind is required to maintain the honour than losing it*…which is immediately followed by:

Upholding 'the state of honour' requires a strong mind and an iron will power. Honour is the reward of such virtues. The most notable example of how hard it is to uphold the state of honour …and, not satisfied with this, you then repeat the thought in the final sentence of the paragraph *They clearly convey the message that it is very hard to persevere in the state of honour.* and that's not all; you go on to repeat essentially the same thought in the first sentence of the concluding paragraph..

(2) The thesis statement is marred by what appears to be an error—a tiny error that in a different situation might easily be overlooked by the reader, or if noticed, would be easily forgiven. However, here, in the lead-up sentence just prior to the thesis statement, accuracy is crucial. Here's what's wrong: Your thesis statement appears to be*: These facts make the state of 'honor'- the state of being respected - so special.* And what are those facts? The first one of the two in the prior sentence is: *It is not hard to achieve it.* Why do you use the word *not* ? If it was a mistake, it is a careless mistake that spoils the effect you're trying to make in the all-important introductory paragraph, and if it was not a mistake but intentional, the word *not* creates a concept that does not match the thought and content anywhere in the essay that follows it.

Suggestions

You could have focused on well-known people as examples. Instead of taking up space with repetitive sentences that give the impression of a lack of planning, you could have written about the honor of a certain political leader as one specific example, and/or also described how another political leader lost his honor through corruptive practices. And certainly you could have shown how a particular saint achieved the honor of sainthood.

Whenever you come across a piece of writing that has as its central theme some aspect of human behavior, but only speaks about it in generalities, such as "people tend to do this or that," and never refers to any specific people as examples to make its point -- you are looking at a piece of writing that's guaranteed to bore you.

The one single promising way to improve your next essay:

Try to make your essay come alive: If the topic has anything to do with people, make sure to include real people in your discussion.

ESSAY THREE

"It is better to die on your feet than to live on your knees" Emiliano Zapata

In the phrase above "It is better to die on your feet" Emiliano Zapata refers to living with a purpose for example standing up for justice/rights no matter what the consequences are. In contrast "To live on your knees" means living without purpose or meaning. I strongly agree with the above comment that it is better to die on your feet as a human being with dignity than to die on your knees with none. I myself have experience what it is like to "live on your knees" and overcome this deep darkness of my life to show why it is better to die on your feet. My sister is an example of an inspirational being that stood up for her rights.

I have experienced what it is like "to live on your knees". I had never felt so belittled and worthless as I did in the first year of my PhD. I found myself alone lost and confused I had hit rock bottom, I had found myself "living on my knees". I woke up every morning and dragged my lost soul in to the university where I performed the same routine day in day out, I felt like I had no purpose. My supervisors had abandoned me. Drafts were handed up that never got a look over; complicated experiments were performed without oversight from my supervisors, I felt lost. Costly experiments repeatedly failed, I felt like my supervisors despised me. As I walked past my supervisor I got shivers throughout my entire body followed by a quick heart rate. I felt like I had failed as a student and let my supervisors down. Endless rivers full of tears and anxiety attacks followed. Anxiety attacks continued. I consulted a councillor we had weekly sessions and I took a leave of absence from my PhD. During my leave of absence my emails were ignored I felt like I had vanished without a trace.

Over time I gradually built up my courage and strength. I reached a point in which I was strong enough to pull myself out of rock bottom. I believed that I am not worthless and I will no longer be belittled by my superiors! I returned to my PhD where I stood up for myself with confidence, I believe that it is better to be true to myself. I consulted my supervisors and told them how they had made me feel how I felt belittled, disrespected and forgotten . I told them how we were no longer working well together as a team and that something needed to change. My supervisors denied that I could possibly feel this way and reviled to me that the team is perfect the way it is. I was shocked, numb and left speechless. How could they not be aware of the way they had made me feel ?

After many days of reflection I decided to leave this team behind and with courage and great strength I moved on, this was very hard for me. I consulted another group within the university who was happy to have me. I finally feel like I have the respect I deserve as a student. Now I no longer feel alone, belittled or disrespected. From this I learnt that I will stand up for what I deserve and I will not be bullied or belittled. This is an example that is close to my heart of how I overcame "living on my knees".

I vividly remember the beginning of my school years for all the wrong reasons. My twin sister found herself confronted with tormenter's day in day out. Her strength was courageous, weeks and months of tormenting went by. We were bought up "to treat others the way you would like to be treated" we lived by this motto. Not once did she show her weakness to the tormenters, she only ever showed grace and ignored everything they said to her despite how nasty it was. By hiding her weakness from the tormentors she tricked them into believing that she wasn't affected by their horrible and hatred comments. Eventually the tormentors gave up. However my sister was left scared. Inside her, emotions had built up and behind closed doors I remember watching the tears roll down her face, it was painful for me to watch this dark time in her life. With many tough weeks of counselling she gained her inner strength back. To this day my sister can stand high as she believed in herself and believed that she deserved better, she stood up for her rights. She is now a huge supporter of anti-bullying.

During our time here on earth I believe that every being should have the right to stand up for what they believe in. No being should ever feel like they are worthless or less important than the people around them, we are all equal here on earth. Very often in life one may reach rock bottom like I did during the first year of my PhD, but this is only for a temporary amount of time. With courage, inner strength and belief we can stand tall "on our feet".

THOUGHT AND CONTENT

Strengths

A good strong effort at writing a reflective essay.

Areas for Improvement

The essay is severely out of balance. In putting the emphasis squarely on the main narrative in great detail, which took up most of the space, you skimped on the essential elements of a reflective essay. The point of a reflective essay is to provide some quality thought about how the experience has affected you, how it's changed your life, how it's reshaped your attitudes and values. You, however, limited your remarks on that aspect to the final 3 lines of Paragraph 4, and a few lines in the conclusion.

Suggestions

If you wish to write a reflective essay, you need to make sure you fully understand the purpose of that format.

You are advised to consult the study guide, The Guru Method, pages 6-23, but especially pages 20-23. It may be that if you did read the portion about reflective essays, you only skimmed it, and missed the point. If that's the case, it's possible that you picked up on the idea that you can write about a personal experience. You may have liked that idea so well that you ignored the sentence that explains the difference between an argumentative essay and a reflective one. It's worth quoting the main point here: "A reflective essay is still an argument….."   Remember that the essay you are going to write for the Gamsat will be weighted about 75% on "quality of thought."

ORGANISATION AND EXPRESSION

Strengths

Aside from the comments, above, regarding your emphasis on detail, if the essay were to be evaluated instead on your writing skill rather than quality of thought, it can be said that the narrative of personal experiences you shared with the reader was, for the most part, quite engaging and evocative.

Areas for Improvement

(1) Repetitive phrasing is annoying.

(2) The inclusion of your sister is confounding, to say the least. A single, brief comment consisting of *My sister is an example of an inspirational being that stood up for her rights* is thrown in abruptly at the end of the introductory paragraph, the whole of which up to that point was about yourself. This reference to your sister then falls into a void; not only is any thought about her abandoned until 3 paragraphs later, but what's worse, inserting this one

sentence abruptly at the end of the crucial introductory paragraph makes for a nonsensical transition to the 2nd paragraph.

Moreover, you treated your sister's experience in the same way as you treated your own: emphasizing the narrative and skimping on your reflections about it.

Suggestions

If you write a reflective essay again, "don't throw out the baby with the bath water." In other words, don't go overboard in the other direction and cut the engaging narrative parts altogether. Emotion is welcome in reflective essays, but it needs to be balanced with the demands of the essay format, which interestingly enough, are very similar in both argumentative and reflectivethat is, both of them must be considered to have an argument, and therefore you must stay focused on what point you're trying be persuasive about.

In order to achieve the balance needed, and at the same time, eliminate the annoying repetitiveness of the present effort, you should plan the essay very methodically before writing down even one word. You should allot a certain block (say, a paragraph) of the plan to the narrative, and then follow up with

the block of a few paragraphs that describe how the experience affected you afterward, in what ways have you changed your attitudes and behaviors, etc..

The one single promising way to improve your next essay:

If that next essay is a reflective one, remember this direct quote from page 21 of The Guru Method: "Understand that some attention to specific details is crucial. However, DO NOT tell stories – they should only serve as take-off points for reflecting on the experience."

ESSAY FOUR

"Honour is the reward of virtue"

Marcus Tullius Cicero

It is misguided to believe that honour can be gained through virtuosity. In fact, virtue has been vastly underappreciated and often persecuted throughout history, and it remains today that virtue is scarcely rewarded with honour, or rewarded at all for that matter.

The Ancient Greeks were amongst the first to contemplate virtuosity and truth, moreover, the philosophers of Ancient Greece contemplated these issues in depth, yet seldom were they rewarded with honour, rather; their attempts to gain virtue and truth led to their alienation and persecution. Socrates questioned the collective notions of justice and the pursuit of goodness and his musings on moral issues were abhorred by those in power. He was subsequently sentenced to death by drinking hemlock for corrupting the minds of the youth and impiety. Often if virtue is not consistent with the status quo it is not only not rewarded, rather it is punished. It is only retrospectively that Socrates has acquired great honour particularly in academia but also to some extent in broader culture.

Virtue has been deemed no more worthy of honour in subsequent centuries following the Greeks. Galileo Galilei, deemed the 'Father of Modern Science' spent the latter part of his life under house arrest as his heliocentric view of the solar system contradicted that of the geocentric view adopted by the theocratic hierarchy of the time. Again honour is only a reward of virtue if it is in tandem with the beliefs held in a society. There is little honour to be gained through virtue, only the honour one can denote to oneself for integrity to his/her beliefs. Galileo is now highly honoured as a genius in the realm of science and revolutionised the study of astronomy as well as various other aspects of physics. However, this honour is again rewarded retrospectively. This has implications for modern society as ideas that seem unamiable or controversial are often extinguished and not honoured, regardless of their truth and virtue.

It would appear that this trend remains to some extent. Many countries still exist under political systems that appear to reward honour to those who have obtained their position arbitrarily. For instance, the monarchy of Britain is a somewhat meaningless figure head rewarded with the utmost honour, yet this is completely independent of being virtuous. Furthermore, politicians are often honoured based on the rhetoric and amiability of their objectives, rather than any virtue they possess. The implications of this are that if we do not honour virtue a body of ideas and beliefs that does not fit the current zeitgeist may be overlooked or even persecuted, only for us to retrospectively look back in years to come and deem that these were in fact virtuous and worthy of honour.

It is an unfortunate truth that people who seek to become virtuous need not expect to be rewarded with honour as history as shown. It appears the virtue of people is much like art in the sense that it becomes significantly more valuable after the person has died and is only rewarded with honour in retrospect.

THOUGHT AND CONTENT

Strengths

This essay features a cogent thesis with a coherent line of thought developed from it.

Areas for Improvement

Your choice of examples to support your thesis that *it remains today that virtue is scarcely rewarded with honour, or rewarded at all for that matter* provides the reader with feeble comparisons between historical practices and those of today, with the result that at least two of your three example paragraphs they are less compelling than you probably intended. In both the social sciences as exemplified by Socrates and the physical sciences as exemplified by Galileo, there are dozens of prestigious awards and prizes granted annually by world-renowned national and international organisations.

Whether you respect these awards or not, the fact that they exist significantly weakens your claim that people in our contemporary society are facing the same opposition as Socrates and Galileo were in their lifetimes, and that they therefore *need not expect to be rewarded with honour as history has shown*. While it is doubtless possible that there will remain some individuals whose ideas *seem unamiable or controversial* and who therefore will not be recognized in their lifetimes, your claim in this essay that such disregard is the rule in contemporary society is not on solid ground.

Suggestions

Beware the pitfall of choosing inappropriate or weak examples to support a position in an argumentative essay concerning contemporary society as a whole. While <u>individual</u> values such a love, hate, desire, ambition, etc., are considered universal and therefore essentially the same today as they are described in ancient scriptures, that is not true for the behavior of society as a whole.

Consider, for instance the case of Galileo you chose as one of your examples: the reason why the comparison just can't be made is mostly due to the fact that we now have instantaneous knowledge of almost everything that goes on around the world, while in Galileo's time it took so many years: first, just for others to establish that he was actually right, and then beyond that, so much time to spread the word.

ORGANISATION AND EXPRESSION

Strengths

The structural framework, in terms of the order in which you present your material, is

basically sound.

Areas for Improvement

(1) The lack of any definition of your key words (*honour* and *virtue)* at the outset is an impediment to the possibility of a quick, smooth read-through.

(2)The lack of mention of any contemporary individuals by name, even though your focus presumably is on contemporary society, is glaring. The only mention that might be considered a reference to real-life individuals is the *monarchy of Britain,* but that's so vague that it hardly counts.

Suggestions

(1) When dealing with ancient terms in a contemporary context, consider defining them to avoid any impediment to the reader's quick grasp of your intent. Although the conventional wisdom—in the context of contemporary English instruction regarding the need for defining one's terms in essay writing— is that it is not generally necessary to define terms that are extremely common, that advice is not applicable here.

This is because the terms *honour* and *virtue*— even though it's more than likely we 21st century denizens have heard or at least seen them used— cannot be said to exist in our everyday lexicon. So, in the present instance, where the understanding of your interpretation of these keywords is essential to the reader's ability to understand your message, combined with the fact that they are words not in common usage today, the reader is left to cobble together what your intent is in the absence of any clarification from you.

(2) Whenever you come across a piece of writing that has as its central theme some aspect of human behavior, but only speaks about it in generalities, such as "people tend to do this or that," and never refers to any specific people as examples to make its point – you're looking at a piece of writing that's guaranteed to bore you.

The one single promising way to improve your next essay:

It's during the 5 minutes you must take for the planning stage before you even write one word: establish your thesis statement with as narrow a focus as possible, and then examine every idea for supportive examples that you think of, filtering them so as to settle on only the few that contribute to the persuasive power of your argument and discarding the rest.

ESSAY TOPICS: TOPIC SIX

TOPIC SIX

Consider the following comments and develop a piece of writing in response to one or more of them.

Your writing will be judged on the quality of your response to the theme; how well you organise and present your point of view, and how effectively you express yourself.

You will not be judged on the views or attitudes you express.

* * * * * * *

Defeat is a school in which truth always grows strong.

Henry Ward Beecher

Making a comeback is one of the most difficult things to do with dignity.

Greg Lake

A man is not defeated by his opponents but by himself.

Jan Christian Smuts

There are some defeats more triumphant than victories.

Michel de Montaigne

Those who are prepared to die for any cause are seldom defeated.

Jawaharlal Nehru

ESSAY ONE

1. "Defeat is a school in which truth always grows strong."

An argument for the triumph of science and fact over belief and rhetoric."

Science by its nature, seeks truth. Human nature however, is not always so accommodating of science when scientific findings conflict with established beliefs. Nowhere is it more true however that "defeat is a school in which truth grows strong" than in the field of science. In the face of opposition from organizations and individuals motivated by belief and agenda, science must continue to counter with fact and evidence for the truth to be accepted by the public and governments.

While there are few people today who would argue the fact that the earth orbits the sun, in the 17th century it was a view that led to the inquisition and house arrest of the scientist Galileo. For Galileo, defeat was a school in which truth, eventually if not his lifetime, emerged triumphant.

Charles Darwin's theory of evolution is another example. Despite widespread, and- in some parts of the world, continued- opposition from religious groups that argue for creationism or intelligent design, theories that rely on religious belief rather than empirically tested findings, evolution is now widely accepted by the public and governments and taught in the majority of schools.

More recently, The NSW Department of Fair Trading ordered the Australian Vaccination Network, an organization that peddles misinformation about links between childhood vaccinations and conditions such as autism, to change its name on the basis that it was misleading the public by not declaring that it was in fact an anti-vaccination organization. The ruling followed a widespread public campaign by health professionals concerned that the scientific truth- that childhood vaccinations are safe- was being overshadowed by the agenda of the AVN. As a result the leader of the AVN resigned and it must now change its name or face being shut down.

The battle for science over belief continues however. Globally, despite widespread scientific consensus on the damaging effects of climate change, Governments, including Australia, have been slow to introduce progressive environmental policies, thanks in part to the continued campaigns of climate-skeptics, groups that claim dubious research to support their belief that human activity is not responsible.

As in battles before, evidence based science must continue to counter belief and rhetoric for the truth to be acknowledged and accepted by the public and acted upon by government.

THOUGHT AND CONTENT

Strengths

Your line of thought is, for the most part, straightforward, cogent, and coherent.

Areas for Improvement

The definition of key words would be a very constructive addition. The words "true" and "truth," as well as "belief" are very central to your argument. Without definitions for these key words, you imply, throughout the piece, that the reader not only knows what you mean when you use them, but that, by further implication, you assume that the reader is on your side in the controversy between what is "true" and what is based on "belief."

Thus, when you speak of *organizations and individuals motivated by belief and agenda* — you appear to be under the assumption that the reader would not be a person *motivated by belief*, and therefore not in need of a definition. And at the same time you fail to acknowledge that those in the "opposition," while likely acknowledging that belief does indeed play a part in their views, would do so proudly, since they consider that very strong belief to be based on "truth" — that is, what is true in their eyes.

Suggestions

You covered the basics. How might you have gone a bit further, in order to make your points more complex, to better reflect the complexity of this perennially vexing problem?

1) Acknowledging the complexity of the problem would add some depth to your thought; it is, after all, the complexity which makes it so difficult for science to make inroads, and for those who rely on "belief" to shed long-held beliefs. And then there is the existence of conflict within the scientist's own mind — scientists who claim they adhere to the scientific method in all things, and manage to make that (which is a belief, after all) coexist mentally with another belief — indeed, a strong belief — in a religion that is thousands of years old (and not based on proven evidence).

2) Another element you could have added to the mix that would enrich the essay is:

you could have shed some light on the differences in the challenges faced by scientists

in earlier times and those in the present. The first two historical figures you mention (Galileo and Darwin) were, although certainly relevant, fighting for recognition in a world long gone (Darwin's observations were made 150 years ago). Comparing their attempts — and the time it took them to gain acceptance with our contemporary scientists' efforts — would certainly add depth.

ORGANISATION AND EXPRESSION

Strengths

The essay is structured properly in terms of flow; it flows smoothly enough for the reader to get a quick snapshot of your thesis and how it is developed.

Areas for Improvement

1) Faulty transition: this is the one major exception to the above comment about structure:

In the face of opposition from organizations and individuals motivated by belief and agenda, science must continue to counter with fact and evidence for the truth to be accepted by the public and governments.

This sentence can be considered the thesis. It is therefore important, and fills the reader with expectation. It comes at the end of a paragraph, and is followed by a new paragraph that is simply jarring, because the transition is not smooth or well thought out. Following on the words of the thesis, one would expect the writer to furnish a description of the current situation, since the thesis is stated in present terms. But instead, you launch into a historical survey. A faulty transition is never acceptable, but it is worse when it occurs right the outset of a piece.

(2) A problem that has already been brought to your attention in an earlier analysis: your failure to demarcate your paragraphs. In order to properly analyze this piece, it was necessary for the analyst to do that work in order to get at least a minimal idea of what you wanted to present. Setting off paragraphs does not mean you can just stop writing in the middle the last line of a block of text, hit Return, and think that you're starting a new paragraph. You have to separate paragraphs by at least a single line space, if not a double line space.

Suggestions

Your conclusion was extremely weak; you simply regurgitated what you'd said in the introduction. You missed an opportunity there to ponder. In an argumentative essay, one of the ways of showing you are a thinking person is to ponder how things might develop in the future. In this case, for example, you could wonder what the effect of instant worldwide communication will have on your topic – will acceptance of scientific conclusions be speeded up, or will higher levels of education worldwide do the trick? This would be more effective than just automatically repeating what you said in the introduction, which is what you did.

The one single promising way to improve your next essay:

Reading a number of published essays will make you much more knowledgeable about the essay format. In addition to textbooks for the study of English language and what you might find on the Internet, another great source for very short essays like this one is the newspaper, where you will find that editorials (on the Op-Ed page) are actually short, usually well-written essays about matters of importance in your world.

ESSAY TWO

"A man is not defeated by his opponents but by himself"

Jan Christian Smuts

Throughout human history in both the world of literature and the actual world that humanity exists in, Smuts' assertion that "a man is not defeated by his opponents but by himself" stands steadfast. By the exploration of both heroes and anti-heroes of the past, it is clear that a fatal flaw in the character proves to be ultimately instrumental in their personally induced downfall.

Pride in human nature, which serves as the source of charismatic leadership testifies in being detrimental by leading the character to overlook potential threats. A pivotal example that clearly demonstrates this is Brutus' dismissal of Mark Antony as a key threat to his safety upon murdering Julius Caesar. Despite Cassius' warnings, he refers to Mark Antony as merely "a limb of Caesar" in Shakespeare's play "Julius Caesar". Consequently, the complacency that arises out of this hubris proves fatal when Brutus' naively allows Mark Antony to deliver a shrewd speech at Caesar's funeral. This culminates in Brutus and his fellow co-conspirators to become the targets of the Plebeian's outrage at Caesar's death providing the platform for the assassins' demise. This ultimately highlights how Brutus' lack of foresight and miscalculations is crucial to his personal downfall.

Lust in the form of adultery is also another universally fundamental factor responsible towards man's personally induced downfall. "The Crucible" by Arthur Miller powerfully embodies this through the protagonist John Proctor's former adulterous relationship with the seductive Abigail. When Salem is encapsulated by a hysterical witch-hunt, Abigail who desires John accuses Proctor's wife of being "guilty". The lack of trust from the souring of Proctor's marriage proves detrimental when he tries to accuse Abigail of deliberate perjury by confessing his adultery. Unfortunately, he fails as his wife Elizabeth who tries to save his reputation contradicts him. He redeems his dignity through this confession. Yet, when the characters in charge of the witch-hunt discover the invalidity of accusations and try to cover up by having Proctor "sign away his sins", he chooses the gallows to save his integrity. Clearly, this is testament to the argument that these series of unfortunate events which culminate in Proctor's tragic but heroic fall can be accredited to the repercussions of his former lust for Abigail that obstructs justice from prevailing in the given scenario.

Greed for political power and domination most important of all illustrates as being the vice in the archetypal anti-hero in all time. Colonel Gaddafi dictator of Libya for forty-two years of despotic rule serves as an ideal example in the exploration of this key trait. The unrestrained Machiavellian measures exploited in the unlawful imprisonment of political opponents in prisons and the ruthless execution of antagonistic forces to the regime is strong justification for sowing the seeds that would sprout his eventual downfall. Yet, most importantly it was his blindness and stubborn refusal for democratic reform in the 2011 Arab Spring rebellions and the brutal demonstration of military defiance to his oppressed Libyan citizens that thrust him into the "dustbin of history". Undoubtedly, the reluctance to share political hegemony and Gaddafi's indestructible narcissism was instrumental in his cold-blooded murder.

Throughout the argument, it remains clear that man is always personally responsible for his own demise regardless of how he dies. Though each individual character's personal traits and experiences differ extensively in both the fictional and real worlds, in the final analysis each of them possesses a unique fatal flaw. This consequently blinds their foresight, entangles them in an unfortunate yet uncontrollable series of events or prevents them from coming in terms with the harsh reality of their imminent destiny ultimately catapulting them to their tragic fates.

THOUGHT AND CONTENT

Strengths

Some creative thought clearly went into this effort to develop and defend your own interpretation of the Smuts quote.

Areas for Improvement

(1) Your effort to support the Smuts assertion is marred by your rather careless shift of focus from the beginning of the essay to the end. By the time the reader arrives at the conclusion of your piece, there seems to be a disconnect between your thesis, as stated in the introductory paragraph, and the conclusion.

Specifically: Your thesis statement seems to be:

By the exploration of both heroes and anti-heroes of the past, it is clear that a fatal flaw in the character proves to be ultimately instrumental in their personally induced downfall. Here, you have clearly delineated your purpose; you've stated that you wish to draw conclusions about heroes and anti-heroes. All well and good; you seem to be indicating that you're wisely limiting your observations to a specific group of people. Nowhere do you say that examples about heroes and anti-heroes will suffice to draw conclusions about characteristics not specific to any defined group, but rather common to all of humanity.

However, when we come to the conclusion, we find this:

…it remains clear that man is always personally responsible for his own demise regardless of how he dies. Now, suddenly, the evidence you provided in three examples of very unusual persons has been transformed into a one-size-fits-all statement of universality! "Man," in the way you use the word in that concluding sentence, refers to all of humanity. Not only that, but "downfall" has now become synonymous with "a tragic fate," and what's more, that "tragic fate" applies to each and every person in this world. This demands from the reader a truly improbable leap of logic.

(2) Lust in the form of adultery is also another universally fundamental factor responsible towards man's personally induced downfall. This extreme statement raises two immediate questions: Who knew that lust in the form of adultery is universal? Or, for that matter, that lust can be considered an element of a person's character —something that is permanent — rather than a desire?

In addition to these aspects, the entire paragraph based on this lust statement is difficult to wade through —a full paragraph devoted to telling a rambling story in an effort to make a point. Rather than contributing to your argument, the entire paragraph actually detracts from it.

Suggestions

Once you've identified your thesis in your introductory remarks, focus on it like a laser beam. Defining your key terms at the outset will help clarify your intent. In this case, it certainly would have helped you develop your line of thought with logical consistency if you had defined, at the least, what you meant by "downfall."

ORGANISATION AND EXPRESSION

Strengths

The essay has structural integrity.

Areas for Improvement

Here is yet another example of the type of florid prose that you have been criticized for using in some of your previous efforts at essay-writing:

This consequently blinds their foresight, entangles them in an unfortunate yet uncontrollable series of events or prevents them from coming in terms with the harsh reality of their imminent destiny ultimately catapulting them to their tragic fates.

Suggestions

Although you have been advised on several occasions previously that sweeping, exaggerated generalities such as the florid one quoted above have no place in essay writing for the Gamsat, you have apparently decided to ignore this advice. It may be that you are unaware of the reasons why that advice has been offered.

Here is one major reason: If you wish to have an opportunity to study medicine, you might take a moment to consider how people working in that profession express themselves in writing: they are extremely guarded. For instance, even if a medical researcher has just completed a study that proves his hypothesis, and he is ecstatic, exclaiming verbally to associates that his new discovery is going to save thousands of lives, nothing of that sort will make it to print.

If he were to submit an article about this research to a medical journal exuding the same sort of exuberance he showed in speaking with his associates, here's just one part of what would happen: In every sentence where the word "will" appeared, that word would be changed to "may." Perhaps this small tidbit of an example will help you understand why your florid language and exaggerations actually work against you.

The one single promising way to improve your next essay:

Focus on the purpose of writing these practice essays in the first place. 75% of the mark will be on quality of thought, <u>so strive to convey that thought with more clarity and less floridity.</u>

ESSAY THREE

"Making a comeback is one of the most difficult things to do with dignity"

Greg lake

The loud rumbling of the train temporarily drowned out my thoughts of anguish and disappointment. We were approaching the last stop, the airport, and as I orchestrated my luggage awkwardly the gaze of other passengers seemed to invoke a sense of pity. Perhaps they could tell from the defeated look on my face, this was not a journey I was going to enjoy.

After the tedium of checking-in I was soon ready to board the plane, prior to which I peered my head up like a periscope in an attempt to get one last, encompassing look at the metropolis of Chicago that lay distantly on the horizon. Upon entering the plane the trademark smell stung my nostrils reminding me immediately of the reverse flight I had gotten over. So full of hope and excitement at the prospects that lay ahead and the seemingly endless possibilities had now dissipated to the point of non-existence.

I was defeated; mentally, physically and financially. The dream of living and working in a different country had over the course of a few weeks become a nightmare due to a comedy of errors, some on my part and some out of my control. My savings to support myself had ran dry before I could find sustainable work, and I now sat on the aircraft wondering meticulously if there was any way I could have prevented this calamity. I felt distraught and somewhat humiliated and wondered how I could remain dignified in front of those whom weren't expecting to see me for the indefinite future.

Touching down on Irish soil my anxieties were causing havoc in my mind, yet I knew I would have to keep my chin up- if only to save face. Several days passed by and I had since 'meeted and greeted' the various friends and family whom weren't expecting to see my face for a long time. Some of the reactions were that of happiness, some of jeering and some of indifference, yet throughout I remained dignified.

I had been completely defeated and felt at an all-time low, it would have been easy to wallow in self- pity, make excuses or place blame. It is extremely difficult to hold your head up high at a time like that, yet it is of crucial importance. On reflection, events that leave you defeated play an important role in the development of your character and what is more important is that you handle such events in a dignified way. Everyone experiences defeat in one form or another throughout their life, yet it is how one comes back from such defeats that allows you to progress and overcome such defeats.

THOUGHT AND CONTENT

Strengths

This is a well-written piece of writing that flows smoothly and tells its story in an engaging way.

Areas for Improvement

Engaging though the telling of the story may be, that is the very element that puts this essay attempt severely out of balance. In putting your emphasis squarely on the main narrative in great detail, which took up almost the entire space, you skimped on the essential elements of what a a reflective essay is supposed to be.

The point of a reflective essay is to provide some quality thought about how the experience has affected you, how it's changed your life, how it's reshaped your attitudes and values. You, however, limited your remarks on that vital aspect to the final 4 lines of the conclusion.

Suggestions

If you wish to write a reflective essay, you need to make sure you fully understand the purpose of that format. You are advised to consult the study guide, The Guru Method, pages 6-23, but but most especially pages 20-23. It may be that if you did read the portion about reflective essays, you only skimmed it, and missed the point. If that's the case, it's possible that you picked up on the idea that you can write about a personal experience.

You may have liked that idea so well that you ignored the sentence that explains the difference between an argumentative essay and a reflective one. It's worth quoting the main point here: "A reflective essay is still an argument….." Remember that the essay you are going to write for the Gamsat will be weighted about 75% on "quality of thought."

ORGANISATION AND EXPRESSION

Strengths

As noted above, the strengths of this essay are in the writing skill. Actually, aside from the comments made above regarding your overemphasis on story detail, if the essay were to be evaluated instead on the basis of your writing skill rather than the quality of thought, you would get high marks for your description of the personal experiences you encountered and your reactions to them. That narrative was, for the most part, quite engaging and evocative.

Areas for Improvement

The criticism of imbalance in this piece of writing extends even to the story-telling itself. That is to say, even if you had been assigned simply to "write about a difficult experience in your life," and not an essay, the story you tell is out of balance. Why is that? Look at all the buildup, the tensions and worries you describe leading up to the plane touching down. And yet, unbelievably, you allow only one single sentence to describe the culmination of all this, to satisfy the curiosity of the reader that you've been building up about what would happen when you landed.

And what exactly was it that you gave the reader to satisfy that curiosity? One single, completely disappointing sentence, quoted here:

Some of the reactions were that of happiness, some of jeering and some of indifference, yet throughout I remained dignified.

Suggestions

If you write a reflective essay again, "don't throw out the baby with the bath water." In other words, don't go overboard in the other direction and cut the engaging narrative parts altogether. Emotion is welcome in reflective essays, but it needs to be balanced with the demands of the essay format, which interestingly enough, are very similar in both argumentative and reflective. That is, both of them must be considered to have an argument, and therefore you must stay focused on what point you're trying be persuasive about.

In order to achieve the balance needed, you should plan the essay very methodically before writing down even one word. In outline form, you should allot a certain block (say, a paragraph) of the plan to the narrative, and then follow up witha few blocks (paragraphs) that describe how the experience affected you afterward, in what ways have you changed your attitudes and behaviors, etc..

The one single promising way to improve your next essay:

If that next essay is a reflective one, remember this direct quote from page 21 of The Guru Method: "Understand that some attention to specific details is crucial. However, DO NOT tell stories – they should only serve as take-off points for reflecting on the experience."

Printed in Great Britain
by Amazon

22013054R00056